C000226953

LEADERSHIP
BEING, KNOWING, DOING

STEPHEN TIERNEY
ILLUSTRATIONS BY STAN DUPP

JOHN CATT

First published 2021

by John Catt Educational Ltd,
15 Riduna Park, Station Road,
Melton, Woodbridge IP12 1QT

Tel: +44 (0) 1394 389850
Fax: +44 (0) 1394 386893
Email: enquiries@johncatt.com
Website: www.johncatt.com

© **2021 Stephen Tierney**

All rights reserved.

No part of this publication may be reproduced,
stored in a retrieval system, transmitted in any
form or by any means, electronic, mechanical,
photocopying, recording, or otherwise, without the
prior permission of the publishers.

Opinions expressed in this publication are those
of the contributors and are not necessarily those
of the publishers or the editors. We cannot accept
responsibility for any errors or omissions.

ISBN: 978 1 913622 92 3

Set and designed by John Catt Educational Limited

Reflections on
Leadership: Being, Knowing, Doing

Leadership: Being, Knowing, Doing is both a position statement and an invaluable manual on the purpose of education. The three Ways of Being, Knowing and Doing with their constituent Basics are a fabulous new lens through which to explore leadership. Each Way (and their Basics), provides depth, definition and direction. Essentially I see this as know yourself, know your stuff and know how to act with an ethical, moral perspective that is so classically Stephen Tierney. Stephen's writing embodies a rich wisdom, deep knowledge and breadth of experience that is compelling. This is a book I know I will be reaching for on many occasions, both for inspiration, for challenge and for direction.

Caroline Barlow, Headteacher, Heathfield Community College

Stephen's third book continues to explore his deep reservoir of knowledge and understanding as to how we, in schools and trusts, lead and how we should strive to improve this area of our work, collectively. The tensions between collaboration and competition are highlighted throughout and the three sections (Being, Knowing, Doing) remind us of what truly matters in the privileged position of leadership, at whatever level.

Stephen's style easily brings together the contrasting roles of the middle leader and the senior leader and draws out the differences between them, and he shows us how they are interdependent. Towards the end of the book, Stephen appraises some of the cornerstones of education policy and makes suggestions for improvement. This is a book you will be pleased to have read.

Jon Chaloner, CEO, GLF Schools

This is a book that very few people apart from Stephen could have written. His honesty about early headship feeling manic through to the intelligent application of research allow the reader to be comforted that they are not alone whilst also knowing that things will improve.

There is no doubt that this book is relevant to all leaders regardless of the 'type' of school, the explanation of how the 'basic' elements all come together when a leader is at their most effective is priceless. Whether an experienced leader or one looking to take their first steps this book will help. I would say the earlier you can get your hands on a copy the better. Whilst you can teach an old dog new tricks it is a lot less painful to start with a clean slate!

Vic Goddard, Co-Principal, Passmores Academy,
CEO of Passmores Cooperative Learning Community

This is a leadership book for our times. Written with great depths of compassion and wisdom. Drawing on his many years' experience of school leadership, Stephen details exactly what it means to lead holistically, with integrity, commitment, passion and purpose. Highly recommended for all school leaders, no matter what stage they are at in their careers.

Viv Grant, Executive Coach and Director of Integrity Coaching

Stephen generously uses his experience and reflections to provide great advice to school and system leaders working through the myriad complexities they face. His division of this book into BEING (who I am and why I am doing this), KNOWING (developing the expertise necessary), and DOING (adopting the most effective behaviours for the context) will prove enormously useful to this generation of school leaders. It is rare to see such a synthesis of reflection and moral purpose with practical tips and advice which is what leaders need now more than ever.

Ros McMullen, founder member of @HeadsRoundtable and co-founder of HeadrestUK, retired Executive Principal, now coaching leaders

This book is 'phronesis' personified. Stephen provides school leaders with a route map of calm amidst ever increasing policy defragmentation.

If I was starting out in school leadership, what I would really need is the personal anecdotes and decision-making process explained, alongside the wisdom accumulated over years from someone who could articulate the complex nature of English education in a pragmatic way; something no online course or education qualification can provide you with. This book provides the cognitive apprenticeship school leaders need, to help move from novice to expert. Understanding why and how is just as important as knowing what. You can know more than anyone, but if you lack the phronesis to implement any of your ideas, you will be lacking as a leader.

Ross Morrison McGill, Founder of @TeacherToolkit, EdD student

A highly topical and relevant guide for education leaders at all levels, informed by professional experience on the front-line. This candid exploration of the frustrations, complexities and triumphs of school leadership – managing competing pressures, juggling multiple priorities and sticking steadfastly to one's moral compass – will resonate with all twenty-first century educators. Stephen Tierney's passion to improve the lives of disadvantaged children is palpable, relayed with humour and humility in a text that will undoubtedly stand the test of time.

Sir Hamid Patel CBE, Chief Executive, Star Academies

Stephen Tierney reflects deeply on leadership through the lens of three core approaches and through eight fundamental 'basics'. He shows great insight about individual, school and system leadership, always illustrating his points with great wisdom and humility. Possibly the greatest insight he offers is 'leave perfection to God'. At a time when school leaders are facing monumental pressure this book provides calm, practical advice and will provide an excellent resource for both new and experienced colleagues looking for inspiration and reassurance.

Dame Alison Peacock, Chief Executive Officer
of the Chartered College of Teaching

I loved *Leadership: Being, Knowing, Doing*. The simple expression of these concepts is profound in Stephen's hands. What stands out for me is a reminder of the key assets on which a leader draws. It was music to my ears to read a brilliant discussion about strategy and the central importance of ethical and moral leadership. This enables us all to aim for equity in education and to succeed collectively. Brilliant!

Vivienne Porritt, Leadership Consultant, Vice President of the Chartered College of Teaching, Co-Founder and Global Strategic Leader of WomenEd (@ViviennePorritt)

When Stephen Tierney was on the frontline of school leadership he was always one of the most authentic voices of reason in the field; always wise, measured and insightful; always honest, principled and pragmatic; always someone who stood up for his beliefs and walked the talk. His new book captures all of that and more. Being. Knowing. Doing. What a brilliant way to capture the essence of leadership. Although rooted in school issues, there's no doubt that this will resonate more widely to other professional domains. The eight Basics are superbly chosen; a truly fresh take on some common challenges. The chapter on Guardianship, for example, provides an excellent insight into what accountability cultures might be. I think serving and aspiring leaders will find this book a compelling read. I see us talking of the Tierney Model in many years to come.

Tom Sherrington. Author of *Teaching Walkthrus* and *The Learning Rainforest*

With the pragmatism, clarity and analytical precision we're used to from Stephen Tierney, this latest work gets to the heart of the joys and challenges of leadership. Drawing on examples from many disciplines and perspectives, Stephen tells honest and relatable stories of leading with knowledge, integrity, curiosity and care.

Dr John Wm Stephens, CEO, Bright Futures Educational Trust

Great things come in threes and Stephen Tierney's third book is, I think, his best. One of our country's most principled school leaders outlines the three strands of his philosophical wisdom in *Leadership: Being, Knowing, Doing*. This book provides leaders new and old with a template for thinking through the challenging situations that face school leaders on a daily basis, peppered with examples of expert decision-making from someone who has been there, seen it, and done it in the toughest of circumstances. This is a must read for school leaders at all levels, at a time when everyone needs as much good judgement and character as we can find.

John Tomsett, experienced school leader, writer and consultant

As always Stephen manages to capture so many important elements of leadership that are both successful and ethical in an accessible yet deeply insightful way. His articulation (and exemplification throughout the book) of 'phronesis' illustrates beautifully what makes his book so useful and practical at the same time as being so much more than 'tips for leaders'. A must read for all in school leadership and those who are contemplating stepping into it.

Professor Samantha Twiselton, OBE – Director of Sheffield Institute of Education, Sheffield Hallam University. Government advisor on all things teacher recruitment, retention and development

This book is for those contemplating leadership as well as those already on this journey. Stephen shares lessons learned throughout his career with humility and wisdom. His focus on listening to and working with the whole school community, especially governors/trustees is a sign of an effective leader. 'Culture matters, because people matter' is so true.

Stephen also shares his thoughts on the issues of 2021 – social justice, ethics, the Nolan Principles of Public Life and the thorny subject of Ofsted. It is an easy and well-structured read with the added benefit of some great illustrations by @StanDupp.

Raj Unsworth, Chair, Member (Greenwood Academies Trust), HR professional, advisor to @HeadsRoundtable

We all know how important good school leadership is, and we all recognise a good school leader when we work with one. What makes them effective isn't just what they know or how they behave, it is their ability to make good decisions reliably. This book is the best I have read in helping leaders make better decisions. In building around ways of knowing, being and doing, Stephen provides a framework that any leader or group of leaders can use to develop and improve.

Jonny Uttley, CEO, The Education Alliance Multi-Academy Trust, Co-author of *Putting Staff First: A Blueprint for Revitalising Our Schools*

Leadership: Being, Knowing, Doing is a book I suspect I will keep on my desk at school so it's within easy reach at all times. It's structured in such a way that I can dip into it for insight, examples, frameworks and links to further reading. By dividing the book into 'being', 'knowing' and 'doing' and then by eight 'basics', each with its own very real example, it has the capacity to support leaders with any of the knotty, persistent challenges they face as well as motivate them to be the best version of themself. In this book, Stephen Tierney effortlessly writes with distinct and deliberate thoughtfulness. Never veering from the goal of a 'life well lived' this feels to me like one of the most 'complete' leadership books I've read because it has both practical, expert examples and resonant, illuminating insights that buzz around in your head a while and then settle in your soul.

Carly Waterman, Headteacher, Lodge Park Academy, Corby

Leadership: Being, Knowing, Doing is an authentic book that brings together research and experience to provide a toolkit for leadership. Stephen's experience of leadership and strong moral compass enable him to critique policy developments and to provide tools for doing the job. He is brutally honest about his own leadership journey and the lessons learnt. Stephen is clear that leadership can be learnt and explores leadership through the basics. Leaders are not perfect – as he writes: 'Leave perfection to God.' This is a must read for all potential leaders.

Sue Williamson, Chief Executive, SSAT

For those who lead.
Become the best version of yourself you can be.
Enable the same in others.

Contents

Foreword

'My hope and intention, in writing Leadership: Being, Knowing, Doing, was to help leaders. Leadership can be learnt. The three Ways with their constituent Basics are a means of exploring leadership. They represent a window or a mirror to help leaders improve their practice. In turn, as leaders, we must support the leaders who follow, who we have a responsibility to intentionally and collectively form.'

The closing paragraph of this book sets out my reason for writing *Leadership: Being, Knowing, Doing.* I started writing it during the first national lockdown in March 2020. Whilst writing, I realised that what I wanted to say about the purpose of education needed a book of its own; hence, publishing *Educating with Purpose: The Heart of What Matters* last year.

This book is structured into three main sections: the Way of Being, the Way of Knowing and the Way of Doing. Each of the Ways has a number of associated Basics, eight in total, which constitute the essence of effective leadership. The eight Basics of effective leadership are: Purpose and Introspection (the Way of Being); Specialism and Strategy (the Way of Knowing); and Implementation, Networking, Guardianship and Expertise (the Way of Doing). Each of the Basics has an initial chapter exploring key leadership themes and an accompanying chapter which provides an example of its application in education. With respect to the Basics of Purpose and Specialism, *Educating with Purpose* may be viewed as a companion book to *Leadership: Being, Knowing, Doing* particularly.

I am indebted to John Tomsett whose invaluable advice and persistence kept my writing true to the structure and ultimately the leadership framework proposed herein. As ever, Malcolm Laverty (@SDupp) has enriched the book with a series of insightful illustrations and provided numerous prompts for me to consider during the writing process. Thank you to the team at John Catt who have edited, typeset and published this book.

Thanks also to my wife, Cath, who has patiently allowed me to write another book. I hope that my grandchildren, who will soon be entering the education system, will learn, grow and flourish under the leadership of the wonderful people who work across the education system. It is to this group of leaders we owe a massive debt and thanks for supporting our children, schools and communities through the COVID-19 pandemic.

Introduction

I arrived to headship with a keen eye for a new idea, a fistful of ready-made solutions and the capacity to work long hours. These allied to Ofsted and Diocesan Section 48 inspections, in my first half year, helped create a one hundred-and-five-page development plan. It led to a manic style of leadership. What the school required was a less frenetic leader and a more phronetic one.

Phronesis is an ancient Greek word for a type of wisdom associated with practical action. It is about good judgement and good character. At its core, it is about the ability to discern how best to act. Practical wisdom involves acting thoughtfully and virtuously and encouraging others to do the same. Virtue, thought and action, which coalesce in effective leadership, I have termed the Way of Being, Way of Knowing and Way of Doing.

Our beliefs, knowledge and experiences form our professional hinterland. These mental schemata operate behind, around and beyond our immediate or everyday thoughts. They profoundly affect our behaviours: the ways we relate to others and how we approach each situation or task. During our careers these schemata grow, often exponentially in the early years of being in a new post.

Here is probably one of the worst marketing slogans ever; this book is limited. It is limited because of and by my finite knowledge and experiences.

Leading a school and then a small trust, in one of the most deprived and disadvantaged areas in England, for two decades, gives a depth to my experience. Too many leaders working in the most disadvantaged areas are long gone before reaching anywhere near twenty years. Prior to this, my teaching experiences were also in deprived areas in the North West of England. Other people may have taught or led in a number and variety of schools in different geographical areas with very different socio-economic intakes. Their experience has greater breadth but more limited depth.

We bring who we are to leadership.

In part, my knowledge of leadership was formed when studying for a Bachelor of Philosophy degree. My research focused on effective science departments. I was interested in why some departments were more successful than others. What aspects of leadership might be most influential and how might I develop them? The research was inspired by a book written by Tom Peters and Robert Waterman (1982) entitled *In Search of Excellence*. The authors had distilled a series of similarities in the ways the most successful companies worked. It fascinated me.

The writers' premise was that the difference between the most successful companies and others was the intensity with which those companies executed the basics. In other words, their success was intentional rather than accidental. Over the decades, I have reflected on the extent to which the preparation and development of school leaders is too often haphazard or at best partial in nature. Far better preparation, induction and on-going training are required. Allied with this is the acceptance that becoming a better leader takes time. It requires the ability and willingness to learn. This includes learning from others and through experience, assisted by the support of an able mentor or coach.

This book is written in the hope that you will find it of value in your development as an increasingly effective leader. That is, it will help you establish and evolve schemata about effective leadership and what the most successful leaders do. It is written from the perspective of experience and guided by the knowledge of others that I have benefitted from along the way. Thinking deeply about the *Ways of Being, Knowing and Doing* will enable you to become the leader you aspire to be and that your community so desperately needs.

Ways of Being, Ways of Knowing and Ways of Doing

The three ways – Being, Knowing and Doing – form a leadership trivium. Trivium literally means the place where three roads meet; *tri* (three) and *via* (road). The Ways of Being, Knowing and Doing are three parts of a whole. The *triquetra*, which I have used as the symbol to represent *Leadership: Being, Knowing, Doing*, has three interlocking shapes that cannot be separated or exist in isolation. Like the triquetra, the ways of leadership must be viewed holistically.

Each of the three ways of leadership has a number of constituent elements. I have referred to these as the Basics, of which there are eight in total. For each of the Basics I will share some of the lessons learnt over the last twenty-five years spent in senior leadership positions in and across schools.

Ways of Being, Knowing and Doing

Ways of Being

Basic 1
Purpose

Basic 2
Introspection

Ways of Knowing

Basic 3
Specialism

Basic 4
Strategy

Ways of Doing

Basic 5
Implementation

Basic 6
Networking

Basic 7
Guardianship

Basic 8
Expertise

Ways of Being

Purpose and introspection are the Basics at the heart of the Way of Being. Pursuing something we believe to be important is intrinsically motivating; it is what gets us out of bed each morning to engage with the world in a meaningful way. Ideally, the purpose of the organisation in which we work and our personal passions should match. When this happens the success of the organisation creates a positive feedback loop which further enhances our motivation. I have always believed in the importance of education as a means to help people have a life well lived. A life in which they enable others to do the same. This is my *telos* or end point of a good education.

Leaders' beliefs about why we educate profoundly affect the organisation's mission, ethos and vision. Purpose may be viewed through the relative importance placed on four educational philosophies: personal empowerment, cultural transmission, preparation for work and preparation for citizenship (Wiliam, 2013). In *Educating with Purpose*, I wrote about these extensively and how they influenced leaders' decision making.

An organisation's history, traditions and values bring it to a certain place in time. It is the responsibility of leaders, working from the root of this place, to chart the forward journey for the organisation. This requires clarity of organisational purpose and a clear understanding of the signs of the time. Each journey sits within a context and community that is, in turn, influenced at a local and national level.

Alongside organisational purpose there is a need for moral purpose. Leaders require a moral compass which directs them towards ethical behaviours. Personal virtues sit alongside the values that deeply influence what a leader believes to be good and right, as they interact with the world.

Introspection is the willingness to look honestly and deeply within. It can be a bruising encounter with the self, and it needs to be done out of love and with love. The aim is to help a leader become the best version of themselves they can be, rather than dwelling on incompleteness and faults.

The Basics of purpose and introspection come from the core of our being, bringing together influences, thoughts and experiences from throughout our lives. They are most exposed at times of greatest stress and are the hardest to change. As matters of character, they are not open to short-term simple manipulation. The Way of Being is fundamentally about purpose – organisational (mission) and moral – and the development of the person and the professional.

As ever, we bring who we are to leadership. Where this authentic self and our actions are misaligned the lack of integrity is easily seen by others. Trust is broken, relationships suffer, and leadership is undermined. Changes in the

Way of Being may be evolutionary or may occur in response to seismic events in our lives, when we are changed by the experience. The 'Great Pause' produced by the worldwide pandemic is one such event, and has deeply impacted on and influenced many people's thinking.

Ways of Knowing

The Way of Knowing constitutes what we have learnt at both an intellectual and experiential level. Specialist and strategic knowledge are the Basics required to lead effectively. Specialism and strategy combine to allow consideration of five aspects associated with organisational improvement and development: content, sequencing, timescales, tactics and responsiveness.

Specialist knowledge enables a leader to engage in the key discourse at the heart of the organisation's mission. This powerful specialist domain-specific knowledge is systemic and context-independent. It includes an expert knowledge of: curriculum design; the organisation of curriculum content; the teaching and learning processes and conditions under which they may be optimised; and assessment.

Strategy is best thought of as a decision making framework (Bungay, 2019). It involves knowledge of how best to act, in order to focus, align and execute work on the organisation's key priorities. These strategic decisions are the linchpin ensuring an alignment and coherence between an organisation's purpose and its enactment. Knowledge of strategy includes an enhanced knowledge of a range of key domains which impact on the organisation's ability to operate as a coherent whole as well as a set of mental models underpinning important leadership behaviours. This knowledge supports the continuation of an organisation's mission within a changing environment. Increasing our knowledge and experience takes time, and specialist and strategic knowledge both develop over the years. They cannot be obtained overnight but may be accelerated by learning with and from others.

In writing *Liminal Leadership*, one of the three bridges I referred to was moving beyond informed to wise. Wisdom – good judgement – is at the root of leadership, and key to wisdom is a way of knowing that is holistic in nature. Western civilisation has evolved with a particular emphasis on the intellect. Cynthia Bourgeault describes knowledge and the intellect as 'A profoundly useful tool for exploring and navigating the world … But the program it runs is perception through separation. It's a grand separating, evaluating, and measuring tool. But it can't "do" because of the limitations built into its operating system.' (Rohr, 2020a)

I sense that some of the difficulties we are currently experiencing in the English education system – and in others around the world – result from too great a bias towards theoretical knowledge of how the system, schools or classrooms should work. This knowledge needs to sit alongside the equally powerful but often more underrated knowledge of experience. Eacott (2008) identified the 'intellectual turmoil' created when models and theories interacted with people. Ideas need to be shaped or moulded by practice, 'the know-how of leadership shaped by practical situations'.

In many ways, thinking is an extremely powerful low risk activity. It is akin to drawing or doodling on a house plan in order to change the internal spaces. For the cost of a bit of pencil lead and a few sheets of tracing paper you can look at multiple different layouts; removing walls with a few strokes of an eraser. It is only when you decide to act that you make a more indelible mark. The cost of knocking down, building, or rebuilding walls – particularly if you have failed to identify which are load-bearing – is much more expensive in reality than in theory. The greater your underpinning knowledge the more profound and beneficial your thinking about what to do will be.

Intellect and experience – thought, application and reflection – operate in an iterative process. The synthesis of theory and action produces a powerful praxis; an iterative forward moving dynamic. In a Franciscan way of thinking Rohr (2020b) stresses the importance of orthopraxy (getting it right in practice; in the doing) rather than orthodoxy (getting it right in theory). However, they are not mutually exclusive. They work best in unison.

The Ways of Being and Knowing form the critical foundations for effective leadership; they are the wisdom that precedes the practice. Experience – at times quite painful – taught me that moving from the privacy of my own good intentions and secure knowledge into the public arena of leadership practice can be challenging, and at times frightening. Ultimately, leadership involves doing and influencing others to act with you. As such, what people experience rather than what leaders intended is key. Getting it right in practice, not just in theory, is the true measure of leadership. Fully crossing the leadership threshold requires a leader to act, as well as be and know.

Ways of Doing

The Way of Doing incorporates four Basics: Implementation, Networking, Guardianship and Expertise. These four Basics interact when leaders start to act, and are the easiest to actually observe in terms of a leader's behaviour. When aligned and operating smoothly they enable the organisation to get better. The greater the alignment and efficiency the quicker this getting better happens. The Basics forming the Ways of Doing are centred on working with and through people. It is leadership focused on: people operating in structures, systems and processes (implementation); people in relationships (networking); people taking responsibility (guardianship) and people empowered (expertise). All improvement work is basically a human endeavour.

Implementation and networking seek to address and remedy challenges faced by the organisation. The former creates the improvement nodes associated with structures, systems and processes which seek to enhance practice. These are the more tangible elements of an organisation. The tacit, almost invisible, network of human connections and relationships ensure these elements work in harmony. Networking (relationship management) requires significant and substantial emotional intelligence from the leader.

The Basics of guardianship and expertise form two sides of the same coin. They are about maximising the potential that exists within the systems, processes and people working in the organisation. Guardianship is focused on setting and improving the standards reached. In the English education system this has unfortunately become part of a low trust, high stakes, cliff-edged, unreliable, high surveillance, inspection style approach. It is too focused on consequences and should be an approach of last resort. Rather, guardianship should primarily focus on assuring quality outcomes through real time low stakes intervention to improve people's practice, as well as the associated systems and processes. Key to this type of work is the creation of feedback loops.

Expertise involves the explicit and coherent development of talent. It requires gains in knowledge and experience – intellectual development and the opportunity to put lessons learnt into practice – in a supportive and reflective environment. These need to be planned for and delivered. Developing expertise requires hard work.

The four Basics making up the Way of Doing are arguably the most amenable to change at a personal and organisational level. It is possible, over time, to act our way towards a new way of thinking and being. Viewing leadership from an action-orientation perspective, what leaders actually do and their impact, Hill and colleagues (2016) identified five different types of leader: accountants, architects, philosophers, soldiers and surgeons. Their research was focused on 'failing schools'; arguably, more correctly referred to as schools that have been let down or left behind (failed) by the system. These schools are often found in the most socio-economically disadvantaged areas.

Over twenty years as a school leader, I have at various times behaved as each of the five different type of leader. I have addressed poor performance, sought to improve pupil behaviour and worked hard to reduce costs. As a new headteacher, walking into a £130,000 budget deficit, I quickly realised that maintaining a balanced budget and focusing spending on staffing and the learning environment was a priority. This went alongside increasing the funding coming into the school, both capital and recurrent. I was fascinated by teaching, assessment and learning, so I led a lot of in-house and external professional development for people, happily chatting about education until the cows came home. Over the years I have led the redesign of structures, systems, processes, buildings and governance. My actions have essentially encompassed all five leadership types. The types are not different people, rather different ways a leader may need to act or react. The same is true of the eight Basics. They are not leadership options, rather the ways of being, knowing and doing which will be called on by all leaders at some point.

Every leader will have certain of the Basics which may be considered strengths; a number may potentially be super strengths. Other Basics may not be as strong. Critically, there needs to be a level of competence within each, a floor standard, if the leader is not to be undermined or struggle for adequacy. The different Basics need to connect coherently to bring a holistic Way of Being, Knowing and Doing. With practice and experience comes an automaticity of leadership which enables increasingly better practice, which impacts positively on the organisation. The different Ways are focused on building and establishing a culture.

Culture matters because people matter; it impacts upon people's daily lived experiences. At its best, culture consists of an organic network of positive, enriching and long-established norms and relationships that govern the way people work, within and beyond the organisation. Culture is not created accidentally. It may be built through deliberate intent – strategy – or relative neglect. An organisation's culture must be contextualised within its domain and aligned with its mission and values (purpose).

Creating the right culture releases the discretionary effort that is required to make a truly great organisation. It aligns and galvanises people; getting them all in the right boat rowing it the same direction. With the right leadership, people get the important jobs done well and in the right way. This is the impact *Leadership: Being, Knowing, Doing* seeks to ensure.

Throughout the book I have, on occasion, used the generic term 'organisation' to include schools, academies, multi-academy trusts and other collaborative structures which bring schools together.

Ways of Being

Basic 1: Purpose

The importance of mission, a moral compass and ethical behaviour

An effective leader is rooted in the history, traditions and values of their organisation. Alive to the signs of the time, they are the custodian of the organisation's narrative – articulating the current mission and ethos – in all they say and do. Working with a wider societal perspective, leaders commit to the moral imperative of enhancing all children's life chances.

Summary

- A leader must possess a clear purpose and moral compass by which to guide the organisation. These must be rooted in the organisation's history and traditions while also being alive to the signs of the time.
- Purpose may be viewed through the relative importance placed on four educational philosophies: personal empowerment, cultural transmission, preparation for work and preparation for citizenship (Wiliam, 2013).
- Purpose matters as it becomes enacted, for example within an organisation's vision, curriculum, pastoral care and support, behaviour system and the professional development offered to staff.
- Signs of the time or mega-trends need to be understood by a leader. Both societal changes and political decisions impact on an organisation's journey. They may be supportive of the direction of travel or not.
- Maintaining a moral compass and ethical behaviour requires constant vigilance and self-awareness. Leaders must seek to act always with integrity, humanity and justice.
- Education must seek to entwine greater social mobility (ladders and sieves) and greater social justice (staircases) as mutually reinforcing outcomes.
- Both social mobility (individualistic, aspiration-focused) and social justice (community, compassion-focused) will be needed to address the increasing issue of poverty in our society.
- The most disadvantaged children, young people and communities need a greater focus on social justice if we are to become a fairer society. One that is more as ease with itself.
- Invariably, when a leader's moral compass strays it is the most disadvantaged and vulnerable in society who pay the greatest price.
- Over time, what appear as small insignificant variations in ethical behaviour add up to have a significant impact. Within education issues of off-rolling and on-rolling signal a loss of moral purpose in some organisations.
- While leaders need to accept personal and professional responsibility for their decisions and behaviours, it is critical to align systems and processes with the moral imperatives and ethical behaviours we wish to see.
- Governance is a means to both promote and protect the mission and values of an organisation; 'People and communities are what matter; not bricks nor buildings'.
- For governance to be successful, a governing body requires a structure and skillset which reflect and embody the organisation's mission and enable it to be carried forwards with integrity.

Purpose

Over a seventy-two-hour period, it was announced, denounced and abandoned, by the six English Premier League clubs. The European Football Super League was intended to be a midweek money maker. Twelve clubs from England, Spain and Italy made up the permanent founding members. It was anticipated that further teams from France and Germany would be encouraged to join with the promise of substantial and stable revenue from the sale of television rights worldwide. After the impact on football finances of the COVID-19 pandemic this additional long-term income made business sense. There would be no more financial vagaries created by the current European football competitions which required a team to earn the right to be included via a successful domestic season the previous year. Promotion and relegation were not factored into the newly proposed super league.

Some of the clubs had American owners who were familiar with – and central to – the proposed franchise style arrangement. Other club owners, concerned about being left behind, signed up with varying degrees of enthusiasm. They knew it would not be an easy or smooth launch, but they were not prepared for what followed. Their new European Super League was met with universal opposition.

The apologies from the football club owners came thick and fast. Central to many of them was the owners' acknowledgement that they had failed to take into account the deep-rooted traditions of the game, the rich heritage of the club and the values at the heart of the organisation. There was a schism between how the owners had behaved and what the fans considered their clubs stood for. The creeping monetisation of football led it to an uncomfortable place; detached from its fan base and history. This episode exemplifies and reinforces the need for a leader to understand the Basic of Purpose. Without a clear organisational and moral purpose, rooted in the organisation's history and traditions, it is too easy for a leader's decision making to become wrong-headed and self-serving.

While history and tradition provide the essential starting point for an organisation, it is the current leader's purpose and sense of mission which creates the potential future trajectory. From an educational perspective, purpose is underpinned by the dynamic tension created between four philosophies:

personal empowerment, cultural transmission, preparation for work and preparation for citizenship (Wiliam, 2013). In *Educating with Purpose*, which contains a fuller discussion and the implications of each philosophy, I summarised the aim of each as:

1. *To develop the potential of the child (personal empowerment). A balance is needed between the acquisition of skills and knowledge, both of which need to be applied. In* Pedagogy of the Oppressed, *Paulo Freire reminds us that 'a person learns to swim in the water, not in a library', hence his focus on praxis (thought and action). Underpinning this is the desire to 'allow young people to take greater control of their own lives' (Wiliam, 2013).*

2. *To pass on 'the best which has been thought and said' (cultural transmission). The focus is almost exclusively on knowledge acquisition and the development of the intellect. E.D. Hirsch Jr (1988) develops a key element with his work on cultural literacy – an anthropological view of education involving 'the transmission to children of the specific information shared by the adults of the group'. This is developed using Michael Young's idea of 'powerful knowledge' (2014), which is more appropriate when considering specialised knowledge.*

3. *To prepare young people for life and work (preparation for work). The focus is on problem solving and real-world experiences. As more educated workers are more productive, there is a correlation between educational achievement and economic prosperity.*

4. *To build communities and overcome social disadvantage (preparation for citizenship). This focuses on the school's context and seeks to support the development of social capital within families and the local community. Key to its success is ensuring young people are sufficiently well informed about substantive and current issues to make decisions and take action in support of the democratic process.*

(Educating with Purpose, 2020)

Purpose matters as it is enacted within an organisation's vision, curriculum, pastoral care and support, behaviour system and the professional development offered to staff. Purpose directs and feeds an organisation's on-going growth and development. As well as purpose, all organisations are significantly influenced by the prevailing conditions in which they exist. These signs of the time or mega-trends need to be understood by a leader. It is for leaders to determine to what extent the current trends help define the organisation's journey or restrict it; operating as either a fair wind and following sea, or a storm to be negotiated. The forces operating on an organisation may be societal or political.

Societal and educational wheels have slowly moved towards greater equality. However, it might take many more generations before we see the fruits of this in greater equity for women, people from BAME backgrounds, people with disabilities and the LGBTQ+ community. There is also a lack of equity for those who are socioeconomically disadvantaged, a characteristic for which there is no protection in law. The long-term disadvantaged continue to have depressed educational and life outcomes.

A moral imperative

Education is a means to produce a more equal and just society. From its inception, mass education has involved a level of wealth redistribution, yet poverty is still a blight on our society. If asked to think about the opposite of poverty, what would you say?

People often suggest words associated with wealth, good jobs and homes. Alternatively, words associated with justice and fairness are proposed. These lead to two different beliefs about what the main outcome of education should be: social mobility or social justice. The former captures the individual aspiration associated with economic independence. The latter incorporates a level of collective compassion related to justice for all in our communities. Laura McInerney (2011) expresses these different views using three metaphors of education: ladders, stairways and sieves. She describes it as 'the basis for almost all educational debate'.

Ladder thinkers see education as the route for climbing to the top of society via a university education. That there is one way up through succeeding in an academic education and the associated examinations. The primary purpose of schools is giving pupils the means to climb the ladder. The route is narrow and individualistic, rooted in the history and cultural norms associated with a ruling elite. Education is a means by which others may enter; mobility through mimicry.

Built on the seven liberal arts of the trivium and quadrivium, and later a traditional curriculum of the classics, university education was a preparation for professions and entry to an upper class. By the 1960s onwards the number of young people attending university had increased, and in the early years of the 21st Century nearly a third of young people attended university, where 'millions imbibed a whole set of values unlike those of their parents or schoolmates' (Hawes, 2020).

Sieve thinkers see education as a way to sift children and young people. The sieve point of view is about 'the right amount and type of education ... to efficiently allocate each person to a job or further study'. For some, the sieve leads to the ladder, for others it leads to a more practical orientated education;

mobility through making. There is a long history of vocational education in England through the apprenticeships and the guilds of the Middle Ages and later the growth of vocational academies in the 18th Century. However, vocational education has unfortunately always been seen as a lesser option by many aspiring parents and young people.

For ladder and sieve thinkers the testing and examination system is critical to their beliefs about education. It is the means by which decisions regarding access to grammar schools, top sets or streams and higher education are to be determined. Examination outcomes provide the crucial passports and means for social mobility. With GCSEs and A-levels being cancelled over recent years, there have been various statements about examinations being the fairest means of assessment. What is meant by examinations being fair, is there is comparability in standards between the grades awarded to pupils in different centres. All pupils sit the same examination papers, containing the same questions for the same length of time.

However, an alternative view is that young people will have sixteen years of vastly different life experiences before they walk into the GCSE examination hall. Examinations essentially ignore the different challenges, opportunities and support young people have been afforded. While there is no perfect system, limiting progression post-16 for disproportionately greater numbers of disadvantaged pupils is something many find unacceptable. Education inputs and outcomes may be viewed from a wider perspective.

Stairway thinkers value diversity in the pathways through education, enabling 'all people to find their strengths and use them to be successful and happy in the future'. Hence, policies favoured by stairway thinkers tend to give a supportive hand to help pupils move from one tread to the next. The desired outcome is based on a quality of life perspective rather than the top goal of a university education. The pupil premium policy is one such enabling policy, in that it aims to help compensate for and equalise the differences in life experiences.

While it would be easy to see these three metaphors as exclusive, competing aims it is preferential to view them as a set of aims which need to be held in tension. Instead of ladder, sieve and stairways thinkers, we need to consider the different contributions and downsides of ladder, sieve and stairway thinking. Both social mobility (ladders and sieves) and social justice (staircases) will be needed to address the increasing issue of poverty in our society. How we navigate these tensions, through the decisions we make, is a critical leadership challenge. It will impact upon the relative priority our actions give to social mobility (individualistic, aspiration-focused) and social justice (community, compassion-focused).

'Political affiliations aside, can we not all agree that no child should be going to bed hungry?'

Marcus Rashford (15 June 2020), in an Open Letter to MPs

Social mobility tends to benefit the middle swathe of the socio-economic spectrum. The long-term poor are often unable to break the shackles of acute, chronic poverty, and for some families poverty has a depth that can be debilitating; economic poverty alongside energy, digital, housing and food poverty. To address this a holistic social justice approach is required if these children and young people are to compete on the ladder or gain greater choice in the sieving process.

Social justice is conspicuous by its absence in much of our history and too many recent policies. The removal of the twenty-pound uplift to Universal Credit, at a time of increasing food and energy costs, will be detrimental to the education of children from our poorest families. There appear to be too few policies that support people out of poverty. A triple lock on the national minimum wage or living wage and Universal Credit would arguably have a significant impact on educational outcomes for many children.

Our data shows it doesn't matter if you go to a school in Britain, Finland or Japan, students from a privileged background tend to do well everywhere. What really distinguishes education systems is their capacity to deploy resources where they can make the most difference. Your effect as a teacher anywhere in the world is a lot bigger for a student who doesn't have a privileged background than for a student who has lots of educational resources.

Andreas Schleicher, OECD

Disappointingly, the Secretary of State for Education in England and the Schools Minister have implemented proposals that will see a significant weakening of the pupil premium policy. Work by Andy Jolley (Twitter: @ajjolley) has exposed the extent of the impact of bringing forward the census collection – from the usual January count to an earlier October count – on the number of pupils entitled to free school meals. The earlier October count will essentially miss all the pupils who became entitled to free school meals between October 2020 and January 2021. Jolley's Freedom of Information request showed that in Greater Manchester 7,231 pupils became entitled to free school meals between October 2020 and January 2021. If the census count had been maintained at its usual time of January it would have realised an additional £8.874 million of pupil premium funding to support children and young people in schools across Greater Manchester. The corresponding figures for London are 18,661 pupils and the loss of £22.769 million of funding. The total loss of funding is calculated by the Department for Education to be £90 million across the country, while the Fischer Family Trust calculates the figure to be £133 million (Thomson, 2021). When the moral compass goes wrong it is invariably the most disadvantaged and vulnerable who lose out. They are least able to compensate for the loss of funding and the opportunities it would have afforded their children.

A moral compass

Returning to the abandoned European Super League, the greater difficulty the whole footballing fraternity faces is that the super league was part of a process, not simply an event. Many of the organisations and clubs complaining – fearing a loss of income, influence and power – had been central to the decision making processes which over decades created some elite national leagues and clubs across Europe. Football fans had previously welcomed the increased financial clout that had enabled their club to buy top players from around the world, on higher salaries than the overwhelming majority of other clubs could afford to pay.

Many small decisions, taken over time, in the absence of a coherent guiding mission and set of values led to the proposed formation of the European Super League. Schools are not immune from similar issues. Maintaining a moral compass and ethical behaviour can be a considerable challenge. It involves integrating various ethical approaches: living as the kind of person we want to be, congruent with the virtues we espouse (integrity); a values-based perspective that supports the common good, the greatest good for the greatest number with a preferential option for the poor or oppressed (humane); and doing what is right (justice).

In terms of values in public life, the Seven Nolan Principles are often referred to: selflessness, integrity, objectivity, accountability, openness, honesty and leadership. The Association of School and College Leaders (ASCL), one of the professional bodies for school leaders in the United Kingdom, established an Ethical Leadership Commission 'because of concerns expressed by ASCL members and others about the lack of guiding principles for ethical leadership in education'. It adopted the Nolan Principles, a set of should and should not statements, adding a series of defined behaviours – personal characteristics or virtues – namely trust, wisdom, kindness, justice, service, courage and optimism (ASCL, 2019).

No matter how comprehensive or worthy, the difficulty with a list approach is that it does not always help you grapple with the inherent complexity associated with the moral dilemmas you face. Words and statements which are 'powerful in the abstract … can be flat and generic on the page. The challenge is always to bring them to life, and into the lives of those who lead' (Kerr, 2013).

To support leaders, I believe the four basic principles of medical ethics are a useful and potentially powerful ally. Sufficiently broad yet focused to hold in tension the complex challenges faced when seeking to determine what is good, they have stood the test of time and found meaning in decisions which are literally life and death. The four principles are:

- Non-maleficence – the call to do no harm or inflict the least harm possible to reach a beneficial outcome.
- Beneficence – the call to do good or promote a course of action that is in the best interests of the person.
- Autonomy – assuming people have the right to make decisions about things that directly affect them; being informed is key.
- Justice – consideration of the impact of individual decisions or decisions about individuals on the wider community or society as a whole.

The final ethical aspect moves the leader to decision making; doing what is right. Difficult decisions must be made even where ethical principles are in conflict, and it is challenging when leaders need to rationalise a given approach, to themselves and others. This is true at a macro level when considering the greater purpose and outcomes of education as well as when making determinations that are more operational in manner.

A moral failure

In England's high stakes education system there are two related ethical issues which are increasingly coming to the fore. One is that some schools attempt to on-roll certain groups of pupils and not others (an admissions issue). The other is the off-rolling of pupils who are in danger of underperforming in public examinations, which is particularly prevalent in secondary schools leading up to GCSE (an exclusion issue).

The underlying ethical issue schools are being challenged with is: who will care for the most vulnerable children and young people in society? This group of pupils is diverse, and includes children who are looked after, those with special educational needs including children with Education and Health Care Plans (EHCPs), those who are long-term economically disadvantaged (of which White British are the largest ethnic group), travellers, and Black/Afro-Caribbean pupils. You would hope that all schools would wish to share in the joys and challenges of educating the most vulnerable pupils. Within reason there would be an equitable share across schools, but this is not always possible. For example, schools are located in geographical areas with very different levels of economic disadvantage and parental choice has to be factored in. However, it is also not always the case even where it is possible.

Stories of some schools suggesting to parents that their child with various additional needs would be better catered for at another school cannot be ignored. While we cannot be certain of the reasons, some odd admission patterns do occur. In a town of seven secondary schools, the 2019 performance tables show one secondary school with the number of pupils on roll as 1168 having 56 pupils with EHCPs. The other six secondary schools with a combined number on roll of 4913 had 79 pupils – in total – with EHCPs. The first school will be required to find £336,000 from its budget, every year, to fund the first £6,000 of the EHCPs. There is no doubt of this school's beneficence.

This is not a moral dilemma, as the ethical way to behave is obvious. Rather there is simply a disconnect between appropriate ethical behaviour and the actions of the few. Sadly, some schools seek to restrict which pupils come on their roll, which is the reverse of how the system should work.

Leaders need to accept personal and professional responsibility for their decisions and behaviours. However, it is also critical to align systems and processes with the moral imperatives and ethical behaviours we wish to see.

> The endgame is to eliminate the need for courage, to render it unnecessary … Success comes when the right things happen by default – not because of individual passion or heroism. Success comes when the odds have shifted.
>
> (Heath, 2020)

While all leaders should behave ethically, some do not. This is the point at which governance must be at its strongest. Governance can be a means to both promote and protect the mission and values of an organisation. It must never be complicit in undermining the common good, or ignoring or covering up unacceptable or questionable practices.

Custodian governors

As part of the Way of Being, the Basic of Purpose – organisational and moral – is at the heart of governance. Governance is part of the leadership network responsible for faithfully taking forward the history, traditions and values of an organisation. It involves looking back at what has been, looking out to what is and looking forward to what could be. This requires senior leaders and governors to work effectively together – each fulfilling their role and enabling the other to fulfil theirs – for the benefit of the organisation and the wider education system.

Throughout this section I have used the terms governors and governing body, they are essentially interchangeable with the terms directors and board.

People and communities are what matter

'Actions not Words' was the motto of the Society of the Holy Child Jesus (SHCJ) sisters. In the nineteenth century, when education for young women and girls was limited, the SHCJ Sisters established a high quality and expansive education for girls, including the arts. For many at that time, this would have been considered a frivolous waste of time and resources, but the Sisters were not for budging.

Sister Maureen Grimley SHCJ, a previous headteacher of the school, helped induct me in the mission and values of the Order and the schools they ran. As with much associated with the mission, values and vision of Catholic education, I was called to be a storyteller not a story writer. The story was written two thousand years ago, and my role was to faithfully lead it during my time as the headteacher. In a fitting tribute to her decades of service, we were able to line both sides of St. Walburga's Road with hundreds of the current generation of pupils to witness Sr. Maureen's hearse on the way to Church. History, traditions and values of an organisation, as embodied by people, need to be recognised and celebrated.

The tradition and values of the SHCJ came to the fore at a critical moment in the current school's development. The governing body, working in partnership with Blackpool Local Authority and Lancaster RC Diocese, were navigating their way through a complex building programme. It would see a £23.5 million capital building programme on the St. Mary's site. The capital programme involved building a brand-new primary school, to replace the original Christ the King buildings, a new parish church and the total refurbishment of St. Mary's including a substantial amount of new build.

As part of the process a public meeting was held in the school's chapel. Many local residents came along. Some were interested in finding out what was being proposed, while others were understandably concerned about the potential disruption during the building programme. Fortunately, some were supportive of the new employment and business opportunities for the local area. One of the attendees was a former pupil who was dismayed that parts of the old building she knew from her time there as a pupil were to be demolished. Her basic argument was the development should only go ahead but only if the old building remained unchanged. Over the decades St. Mary's had become a Hogwarts style labyrinth of additions that lacked accessibility and legibility; even as the headteacher, there were times I got lost.

As the meeting progressed, I did my best, alongside the architects and local authority officer, to explain the rationale for the proposals. Sat quietly in the middle of the chapel were Sr. Philomena Grimley (Sr. Maureen's sister) and a few members of the SHCJ community. At just the right moment, Sr. Philomena stood up and in her quiet, affirming and generous way informed the meeting that the SHCJ sisters were happy for all the buildings to be knocked down or changed to suit the needs of the current pupils and their education. It was a transformational statement, and the message was loud and clear; 'People and communities are what matter; not bricks nor buildings'. This was the SHCJ's mission and what it held dear when difficult choices were to be made. It was our mission too. The Sisters had successfully imbued the next generation of custodians with their founding spirit. As leaders, we build on what comes before us.

Key to leadership is the interpretation of the history of an organisation and its foundational traditions, principles and values that may be used to help guide the onward journey – to recognise what is substantive and what is peripheral – and to then apply them to the current context and times. Alongside the need for governors to be the custodians of the past they also need to be able to chart a way forward for the organisation. It is a key part of what they do. On many occasions the forward outlook, generosity of spirit and deep sense of mission of the SHCJ, which called us to action on behalf of our young people and their communities, inspired our decisions as a governing body.

Creating synergy: matching form and function

For governance to be successful it needs to form a competent legal entity. This requires a structure and skillset which reflects and embodies the organisation's mission and enables it to be carried forwards with integrity. Over two decades leading schools, I worked as part of a range of governance structures. Initially, it was a single school with its own governing body. Our voluntary aided status meant the majority of governors were foundation governors appointed by the Bishop (Diocese), and in addition there were staff, parent and local authority governors.

As my career developed, I started thinking and working at a bit more of a system level. The 'one school – one governing body' model seemed increasingly limited in terms of linking together a governance structure with a way of working. Sir David Carter puts it eloquently when he says, 'No single school has: all the answers; a monopoly on challenge; capacity to solve all of its challenges on its own; or should be content if they see another school in trouble.'

For many of the reasons above, in January 2009 we formed a hard federated governing body with the local Catholic primary school, Christ the King, which bordered our playing fields. There was now one governing body with responsibility for both schools. In keeping with our values of partnership, the governing body was extended to nearly thirty so that all the original governors could be included on the newly formed, hard federated governing body. Meetings were difficult due to the large numbers, but over a relatively short period the governing body reduced to twenty-four and then twenty members, as people stood down or their term of office came to an end. This governance structure was now aligned with the vision of deep partnership work. Despite this, the schools operated largely autonomously.

You see similar ways of working in many multi-academy trusts. Schools come together as a single legal entity but continue to work separately. This may be supported by a *devo max* approach with considerable delegation of authority to local governing bodies. For some trusts or groups of hard federated schools, the autonomy works well even if it does not maximise the potential for working together. In other situations there can be infighting, with one school making a unilateral declaration of independence or even conducting a *coup d'état*. The autonomous functioning of the headteachers is misaligned with the governance structure, and at some point the tensions created by a misalignment of structures and purpose are likely to reach a breaking point.

When the Diocese established a multi-academy trust to support one of the local Catholic primary schools that had fallen out of favour with Ofsted, our governing body was committed to supporting its development. We believed it must work on the basis that we were coming together to work together. St. Mary's and Christ the King schools had started establishing ways of supporting each other in a closer working relationship. This included a number of joint appointments, which was so much easier as the schools had the same employer; their shared governing body.

The three schools that formed the multi-academy trust were not looking for standardisation but accepted that they would need to surrender some of their autonomy to align key aspects of their work. In keeping with our belief in deep partnership through greater alignment, the Trust's board was established with no local governing bodies, as the latter were felt to be unnecessary. In part, the small size of the Trust and the close geographical clustering of the school allowed this to work well, although as ever, it was not for everyone.

The third Thursday in January

Alongside the work the governing body does on organisational purpose it must also be the custodian of the values – the moral purpose – of the organisation. School leaders need to provide information in the right format – neither too little nor excessively complex – on a range of issues for the governing body to make informed decisions on. Governors need to be good at checking the detail, asking the right questions and interrogating potential statutory, technical or ethical breaches. One area governors need to give far more consideration to is the issue relating to the excessive movement of pupils out of the school; the off-rolling issue I referred to in the previous chapter.

The third Thursday in January is significant. It is the date of the census that determines which Year 11 pupils the school will be held accountable for in the GCSE Summer examinations. The pupils' results appear in the performance tables the following academic year, and for all pupils on roll at this point in time, the school – and consequently the school's leaders and teachers – will be held 100% accountable. This is irrespective of whether the young person started the school in Year 7 or arrived in Year 11 the week before the January census, having been educated for over four years at one or more other schools. It is yet another feature in education that fails the common sense test. There are far too many perverse incentives for the unscrupulous, the fearful or the uninformed to knowingly or unknowingly game the system.

Ofsted belatedly woke up to the issue. Unfortunately, the inspectorate's attempt to stop off-rolling showed a naïve understanding of the problem. It was more a view from the ivory tower than an understanding of what is happening on the ground. Lest you think I am being harsh, imagine the following scenario: two schools in the same area with almost identical intakes and above national average levels of disadvantaged children.

School A has had, on average, two or three permanent exclusions a year over the past five years. Given the number of adverse childhood experiences so many of its young people have experienced, it took a particular approach to pastoral care. For the relatively few, deeply troubled, high needs pupils, it supported them through their difficulties at a personal, social and emotional level to great effect. It took money, time and the patience of a saint, or in reality many saints, to get these pupils through to the end of Year 11. Despite all this, these pupils achieve limited academic success at GCSE. The school retains 100% responsibility for these pupils in terms of accountability. Over the years, performance tables and Ofsted have not always been kind to this school.

School B takes a different approach. The school's no exceptions, no nonsense, consequence or reward system has led to twelve to fifteen pupils being permanently excluded each year over the past five years. In total, there were between sixty to seventy-five pupils the school is no longer held accountable for. Permanently excluded young people are predominantly those with low prior attainment, the economically poor and those with special educational needs and disabilities (Nye and Thomson, 2018). None of these young people will appear in the school's examination results. They were all permanently excluded before the third Thursday in January of their Year 11. The national peak in Summer Term Year 10 and Autumn Term Year 11 of permanent exclusions is reflected in the school's data. Unsurprisingly, the performance tables and Ofsted laud the school's high quality of education.

In its most recent update to inspectors, Ofsted has stated that inspectors must use the term 'off-rolling' where it has evidence it has occurred (Roberts, 2021), but it is too little too late for too many young people.

The poorest in our society often lack the capacity and in some cases the capability to navigate the unfamiliar and frightening quasi-legal processes associated with permanent exclusions. Add to this the rising numbers of secondary pupils entering elective home education, sometimes more at the behest of the school than the family, or pupils and parents under pressure to move their child to a different school. There is always a school at the bottom of the local food chain, with spaces in year groups, that has to accept any pupil who turns up for admission. The system is allowing, even driving, the wrong behaviours. When this happens, leaders need to be brave enough to do what is morally right. Governors are there to ensure that they do and reassure them of their continued support. This is part and parcel of the required working relationship.

Over the years, I have benefitted from the support of a governing body that did not overreact to every bump in the road. Rather, it looked at what had been accomplished over time; what improvements were being put in place and how effectively senior leaders reacted to setbacks and problems. On a number of occasions they set up short-term single issue scrutiny committees – for example on attendance of pupil premium pupils – alongside their established committee structure. These governors challenged and supported in an effective and balanced manner.

The awkward governors

It is important for the headteacher and governors to develop positive working relationships. However, this should never reach the point where the governing body becomes overly compliant and tends towards agreeing with or accepting pretty much everything the headteacher proposes. A lack of challenge can lead to underperformance not being addressed or poor decision making at a strategic level. This will cause the organisation to move in the wrong direction, fail to move at all or move forward in a less than effective manner. The converse of this is where an antagonistic relationship forms between the governing body and the headteacher with either one or both parties believing they are being undermined by the other. Needless to say, in these situations the functioning of both the governing body and the headteacher will be sub-optimal.

Governance is a corporate structure where no single individual can act unless specifically mandated to. It is a governing *body*; it acts as one. Where an individual governor is behaving in an inappropriate way – the signs tend to be many other governors complaining about the individual or their actions, or talking about resigning from the governing body – it is a matter for the chair of the governing body, potentially supported by the clerk. Discussions can be helped if the governing body has adopted a code of conduct. The National Governance Association has an excellent one on its website that we adopted each year, which provides clear and useful guidance

Over two and a half decades of involvement with governors, I can only think of two governors who I would describe as awkward to the point of damaging the functioning of the governing body. The line between challenging – something a headteacher should expect and welcome, no matter how uncomfortable – and someone being deliberately or unwittingly disruptive can be a fine one. As a headteacher, it is worth asking, are they really being awkward or just asking the questions that need to be asked?

Often the awkward behaviour stems from a failure to understand the role. No governor is a representative of a particular group; a governor's role is to bring a particular perspective – parents, staff, local authority, diocesan – to inform and enrich discussions and decision making. In meetings it is important to avoid individual governors riding hobby horses or constantly saying 'I've had a conversation with a parent/member of staff who are not happy about ...'. There are separate policies and procedures to deal with these issues. Such issues may be more legitimately considered by using complaints or grievance policies. The early stages of these procedures involve people talking about their concerns in an informal manner, in order to reach an understanding and solution to the issue. The specific issues should not be discussed at governing body or governors' committee meetings. Firstly, this is not the purpose of those meetings. Secondly, if policies and procedures are enacted there may be a need for 'untainted' governors to sit on panels, including appeals, at a future date.

The behaviour of the two awkward governors I encountered stands in stark contrast to the commitment and longevity of the hundred-plus selfless, committed governors I worked with over eighteen years as a headteacher and latterly a CEO. In my resignation letter of February 2019, I wrote to Barry, our longstanding Chair,

The opportunity to have such an enjoyable and fulfilling career has been, in no small part, due to the governors and directors who I have had the privilege and pleasure of working with. I am indebted and grateful to them all. I realise there are a number of current Directors who helped appoint me and will be eternally grateful for the opportunity they afforded me.' It ended, *'With thanks for your friendships, support and challenge over the years.*

Effective governance requires skilled and committed people. I was fortunate to work with so many over the years.

Basic 2: Introspection

The importance of reflecting on your intentions, capability and impact as a leader

An effective leader understands the need to look honestly and deeply within, identifying personal strengths on which to build and weaknesses to be addressed. Seeking to become the best version of themselves they can be, they commit to continuous improvement as both a journey and destination.

Summary

- Authentic leadership is an extension of self. Becoming a more rounded and complete leader often requires us to become a better person first.
- Being aware of your behaviours is a start. Doing something about maintaining, adapting or stopping different behaviours, as appropriate, is part of the progression towards more effective leadership.
- Leaders must hold in dynamic tension self-confidence and self-doubt in order to ensure the necessary humility required to effectively lead an organisation. Part of maintaining this balance is to spend time in personal reflection; time sitting on the mountain top.
- The mountain top provides an important perspective for a leader. It helps them reflect on how and whether the daily operational work of an organisation is aligned with its deeper purpose.
- The leadership journey requires a leader to develop a sense of self, a relatedness to others and to find a greater meaning that brings purpose to their lives.
- Three stages of leadership are characterised by: personal competence; empowerment of others in the organisation; and recognising the interdependence and connectedness of all educators for collectively ensuring children's education and well-being.
- Worrying can be an exhausting and unproductive emotion if not channelled effectively. Invariably much of what we worry about does not come to pass, has far less impact than initially thought, or can be mitigated.
- Effectively channelling our concerns involves a process of rationalising the emotional: to what extent are the worries or concerns likely to happen and what impact might they have?
- Concerns may be analysed through four different lenses (factors): likelihood, quantum, longevity and scope.
- The process of risk assessment takes the worries and concerns from inside and moves them to a place where they can be viewed, interrogated and ultimately acted on. This gives a sense of empowerment; being in control of events rather than at their mercy.
- In looking at ways of mitigating various worries and concerns, it is often important to break them down into their constituent parts. This can move something from appearing overwhelming to bite-size issues that may be acted on.

Introspection

In *Legacy*, a book about the rebuilding of the New Zealand All Blacks rugby team, Kerr (2013) tells the story of Vince Lombardi. Lombardi was employed as the coach of an underperforming Green Bay Packers American football team. He developed the Lombardi Model which started with the simple statement, 'Only by knowing yourself can you become an effective leader'. The Green Bay Packers went on to win successive Super Bowls, the pinnacle of the American football season, in 1966 and 1967.

Lombardi was concerned with the personal values that formed the basis for character development and consequently integrity, from which came leadership. Lombardi saw character formation as key; 'and character begins with humility'. It is this humility that leads the international All Blacks players to continuously ask the question 'How can we do this better?' about themselves as players and as a team. Becoming a more rounded and complete leader often requires us to become a better person first.

Authentic leadership is an extension of self; patterns of behaviour you see in your personal life will be mirrored in your professional life and *vice versa*. Leadership is not something you simply switch on and off at work. It is important to understand who you are; in all your complexity, contradictions and incompleteness. Your true self is often most exposed at times of greatest stress. Under stress, I had a tendency to add just one more task on to my To Do list, a couple more meetings into my already overfull diary, another objective to the school development plan, and so it would go on in an increasingly frenetic existence.

Being aware of your behaviours is a start. Doing something about maintaining, adapting or stopping different behaviours, as appropriate, is part of the progression towards more effective leadership. It is about both self-awareness and self-management (Goleman *et al.*, 2002).

Public confidence, private doubt

One of the blogs I wrote, *Learning to Live with Leadership*, was constructed around the phrase 'You will spend longer worrying than you do working'. Even when I stopped working for the day I struggled to switch off. Work that still needed completing, concerns and potential solutions, or new ideas would continue to bounce around in my head. People sometimes told me to stop worrying, to which my response was usually *'But it is the first line of my job description'*. Going into headship, people tend to worry about managing budgets and personnel issues, but over the years, these were not the ones that kept me awake at night.

Too often, lying awake in the early hours of the morning, I would be worrying about the potential nightmare consequences – personally and for the organisation – of an adverse Ofsted report; how to deal with the fallout of a pupil whose multi-coloured hair was in breach of the school's uniform code; an architect's design for a building with too few walls between classrooms. Over my career, I worried a lot.

I still sometimes reflect on decisions I made over the years. Some were controversial at the time, others not so. This worry is part of the private doubt of a leader's life; it is why introspection is a Basic within the Way of Being. This private doubt counteracts overconfidence, arrogance and hubris, which are the enemy of introspection, producing a false self-assessment of capabilities and impact. They may also distort a necessary sense of empowerment, mutating it into a sense of entitlement (Laker *et al.*, 2021). Or worse still, a belief that the laws, standards and norms, which bind us together as a coherent organisation or respectful society, no longer apply. Arrogance, hubris and a sense of entitlement may disproportionately affect the affluent, particularly affluent white men who may have no counterbalancing experience of discrimination. It is important to differentiate between 'on average' and the individual. Individuals may vary significantly from the average. Anyone can be prone to a lack of humility.

Yet out of the private doubt must come the confidence to make decisions and act on them in the public arena. Part of maintaining what can be a fine balance of confidence and doubt is to spend time in personal reflection or reflecting with the help of a mentor or coach.

Sitting on a mountain top

When appointed to the headship at St. Mary's in 2000, one of the final questions the governors asked me was 'What would you need from/expect of us?' In all the preparation I had done, thinking about various questions I might be asked and what my response might be, I had not anticipated this question. My response was probably not that coherent but one aspect of it I have always remembered.

I told the appointment panel that governors would need to understand that on occasion I would require time to 'sit on a mountain top'. I now warn groups of leaders never to work for any organisation that does not understand their need to sit on the mountain top or prevents them from doing it. The idea of sitting on a mountain top is rich in symbolism and has an important root in faith. From Moses receiving the Ten Commandments, the Sermon on the Mount to the transfiguration of Jesus, a lot of important events took place on a mount. What I said lacked the importance of these events, but it is likely to have resonated with the panel.

Sitting on the mountain top provides a greater perspective, and perspective is important to a leader. Within the confines of their more operational work, it is easy for leaders to lose sight of how their daily work and that of others contributes towards the greater purpose and vision of the organisation. It also allows you time to shoot an azimuth. In general terms, shooting an azimuth is used to describe the process of climbing to a high position and spotting a series of objects or landmarks that may be used to navigate towards a chosen destination. If you allow it to, the mountain top will help you see a greater purpose to your work, ways to move forward and provide the space to reflect on the contributions you have already made, and those you can still make.

It is important to sit on the mountain top; to take the time to reflect, ponder and contemplate. It is not another task to do but rather an opportunity to just be. You see the vastness before you and appreciate your insignificance. The mountain top is a place of humility. It is also a private space where a person may think, reflect on their experiences and reform their knowledge, giving them new insights and ways of thinking. It is a place to look back and reflect in order to move forward. As one of the Basics of the Way of Being, introspection must not be self-serving but rather a means by which the beneficial impacts of our leadership may be improved and the harmful effects reduced. This involves being clear about our purpose and intentions, and seeing through the most important aspects of our role.

Leaders need to find time for themselves. In a busy schedule it is all too easy to prioritise the task in hand and the well-being of others. Covey (2004) refers to the need to 'sharpen the saw'. In response to the suggestion that the exhausted person take a moment to sharpen their saw, they responded 'I don't have time to sharpen the saw, I am too busy sawing!' This is the point at which servant leadership turns to pointless martyrdom. An exhausted leader is useless to themselves, their colleagues and the organisation.

Alongside others during the pandemic, school leaders have experienced a time like no other generation of school leaders has ever faced. Many are simply exhausted; running on empty. The nearest I came to this was over a four-year period when we were part of the Building Schools for the Future programme. We were building a new primary school on site, which incorporated a new church into the design, and towards the end of the build, we needed to establish a multi-academy trust. Four years of working 60-70-hour weeks and losing holidays to contract negotiations, left me exhausted and clinging on by my fingertips. Later my PA, Anne, shared with me that staff used to come and ask her 'Is he in a good mood today?' She would answer, 'He hasn't been in a good mood for years so you might as well go in.' There is a need for all leaders to refill their own reservoir if they are going to be able to help and support others.

There comes a time when you need to look in the mirror. You may not always like what you see, but forgiveness of self is a critical component of introspection. There may often be a lot to forgive, as none of us is perfect as a person, leader, partner, parent, child or friend. We need the time and space to reset ourselves to the best version of ourselves that we can be. In part this is about a process of reconciliation; the rebuilding of relationships with others. A key aspect of this is committing to not making the same mistakes time and time again. We need to learn new ways or more often follow through on what we know is right.

The other part of this reset is to reconnect to the deeper purpose of why we came into the profession and chose to become a school leader. There is a need to re-align what we believe with what we are doing. It is the melding of knowledge, experience and emotions which enables us to make decisions which we *think* are right and which *feel* right. The Basics of purpose and introspection are entwined parts of the Way of Being. There may be the occasional epiphany on the mountain top but more often than not it is a process of gradual growth, which requires personal development alongside professional development.

In writing *Liminal Leadership*, I shared the leadership reference form we used at that time. It was based on a document called *Rush to the Top* from the Hay Group (2007). As well as using it for references, I also utilised it as part of a self-reflection exercise for future senior leaders on a number of in-house courses, as a means for them to identify their strengths and potential areas for further development. One of the three sections was concerned with emotional intelligence and resilience.

Area	Outstanding	Very good	Sound	Area for future development
Self-Awareness	Very aware of own strengths, areas for development and emotions.	Aware of own strengths, areas for development and emotions.	Aware of some strengths, areas for development and emotions.	Has difficulty seeing own strengths, areas for development or emotions.
Self-Control	Effectively controls emotions even in stressful situations.	Effectively controls emotions in most situations.	Normally in control of his/her emotions.	Needs to show greater self-control in some situations.
Empathy	Adept and able to see the value in many different viewpoints. Relates well to others.	Able to see the value in many different viewpoints. Relates well to others.	Able to see the value in different viewpoints. Relates well to most other people.	Able to see different viewpoints. Relates well to some people.
Influence	Has significant credibility with staff who value his/her input.	Has credibility with staff who value his/her input.	Is developing credibility with staff who are beginning to value his/her input.	Needs to further develop credibility with staff.
Emotional Stability	High resilience and effective performance in difficult, pressurised situations.	Shows resilience and effective performance in pressurised situations.	With support shows effective performance in difficult situations.	Needs personal support and assistance in difficult situations.

There is a need for accurate self-assessment as part of the process of personal or professional development, it is an essential aspect of self-awareness.

Steve Munby's 2019 book, *Imperfect Leadership*, is a great example of the self-awareness needed by a leader. Understanding his limitations led to him identifying a number of mentors to help him develop as a leader. During his time as the CEO of the National College for School Leadership, he concluded, 'the chances of someone who lacks self-awareness becoming an effective leader are very small'. This led to revised entry criteria for the National Professional Qualification for Headship in 2008, with a much greater focus on self-awareness. I undertook the qualification prior to this change, but I can attest to the integral nature of self-awareness and reflection in the Leadership Programme for Serving Headteachers. Completing the programme four years into headship, it was one of the most formative programmes I had ever been part of, with 360-degree leadership reviews and peer to peer discussions throughout. I always felt it was a shame that I had not been allowed to undertake it earlier in headship, or arguably prior to coming into post.

Up to that point in my career I had been honing various generic and domain-specific knowledge and skills, primarily using my cognitive abilities to get the task done, which had arguably brought me much success. Looking inside – I mean deep inside – at the person you are when getting the job done can be both uncomfortable and affirming. Misquoting Steve Chalke, 'It's not just what we do as leaders that matters but who we become while we are doing it'. People sometimes refer to it as the eulogy moment. What will people remember about you as a leader once you have gone?

Our growth and development as a leader has much in common with our growth and development as a person. Over our lifetime we need to develop a sense of self, a relatedness to others, and to find a greater meaning that brings purpose to our lives. Like a set of Russian dolls, each layer may be opened up to reveal another deeper layer within. I often talk about the three phases of headship that help describe my own leadership journey. At the interface of each phase there was a sense of dissonance between what I was doing and what the school required. It took time and effort to transition from one phase to the next. The need to spend time reflecting on my Way of Being – the introspection when sitting on the mountain top – was critical to me moving on.

The early phase of headship was about establishing personal credibility and starting the process of visioning, to give the organisation direction and a fresh impetus. There was a lot of 'I' in the leadership. A bringing of the values I held; what I valued in education; alongside the knowledge and experiences I had acquired over the years. While this is not necessarily a bad thing it is an insufficient thing. It is dangerous to only view the world from the limitations of self. Some leaders can get stuck here and fail to recognise the wisdom the school staff and local community can bring. The challenge is how to move genuinely towards the greater engagement of staff, children and young people, parents and the local community while maintaining a sense of direction.

Moving beyond simply listening to the staff, pupils and local community to empowering them was the major change that took me into the second phase of headship. This involved empowering people in order to actively engage them in forming and taking forward the organisation. It involved giving away power and influence while still managing meaning for the group; holding tightly to the *why* but giving greater ownership of the *what* and *how* to others. This helps develop a greater sense of belonging and trust within the group, which is a good thing but again it is insufficient. Leaders who stop or get stuck here may spend their time defending or isolating their organisation, too often to the detriment of themselves and others.

The final phase was about system leadership. It was about recognising the interdependence and connectedness of all educators, alongside individual responsibilities. Taking responsibility for the lives well lived of all our nation's children and young people, not just those with whom we come into daily contact. Vivienne Porritt (Brennan, 2013) has a lovely expression; 'the goalposts move, the goals remain the same'. It reminds us that while successive governments or individual leaders may try to shift priorities, there is a deeper truth about why we educate: the empowering, acculturation and preparation for work and citizenship of all our society's children and young people. This is no longer about ourselves or our schools. We succeed collectively – for all our children – or not at all.

The need for self-awareness – recognising your emotions and their impact; your strengths and limitations and a sense of self-worth – is critical to the leadership journey. It helps develop and facilitate self-management, and this involves putting the time sat on the mountain top into practice. The Basic of Introspection is a *must do* rather than a *nice to do* aspect of leadership.

What keeps you awake at night?

In the previous chapter I mentioned it wasn't the hours I worked, it was the hours I worried. This was nearly always my greatest challenge. Worrying can be an exhausting and unproductive emotion, if not channelled effectively. A lot of things I worried about were relatively small issues, although occasionally my worries were about things of greater significance. Invariably much of what I worried about did not come to pass, had far less impact than I initially thought, or I managed to mitigate the concern in some way.

Effectively channelling our concerns involves a process of rationalising the emotional. To what extent are the worries or concerns likely to happen? What impact might they have and which of these worries may now be left to one side or acted on to mitigate? Analysing concerns through four different lenses is a part of the introspective process. The four analytical lenses (factors) are: likelihood, quantum, longevity and scope. It is an approach often used in risk management. Each factor should be scored on a scale of 1 (low) to 4 (high).

The likelihood is a simple assessment of whether something will happen or not, which might be certain or almost certain (4), probable (3), possible (2), or unlikely (1). The quantum is an assessment of the size of the impact on the organisation. It might be game-changing and impact on the organisation's ability to continue to exist or function effectively (4). Alternatively, the quantum might be viewed as significant and substantial (3), moderate (2), or limited (1) in terms of the size of the impact. Closely associated to this is the longevity of the potential consequences for the organisation, and whether the impact and the fallout will be felt for years (4), months (3), weeks (2), or days (1). Finally, it is worth considering the scope of the impact, in what I would term a range from personal to personnel.

Some of the things that keep us awake at night are associated with our own relationships with others at work. These are not unimportant but need to be differentiated from issues that are likely to affect people across the whole organisation. Due to the very personal nature of the former we can conflate and entwine it with the latter, and we need to be honest with ourselves as we assess this risk. Its range may vary from an impact on all or nearly all people in the organisation (4), large groups of people, for example all teachers, or support staff or pupils (3), smaller groups (2), or individuals (1). By recording the scores for each factor – the different worries that are keeping you awake at night – you can begin to identify those issues of greatest concern.

Worries/Concerns	Likelihood	Quantum	Longevity	Scope	Total
Least significant	1	1	1	1	1x1x1x1 =1
	2	2	2	2	2x2x2x2 = 16
	3	3	3	3	3x3x3x3 = 108
Most significant	4	4	4	4	4x4x4x4 = 256

By multiplying the scores for the four different factors together you will obtain a total score from 1 – 256. It is important to look at the overall order or rank of the concerns, as scored, and check this against your gut feeling. Does the relative order of the different concerns feel about right? Are you more able to rationalise – due to the likelihood, quantum, longevity or scope – why some of the concerns are of greater importance than others? The table shows the range of scores but there is no set cut off-point or point at which to act. The scoring process merely feeds into a leader's more intuitive decision making process. At this point there is a need to decide what actions need taking.

The process above may also be used with a team or group and is equally effective when looking at a range of potential development priorities to identify the few which will have greatest impact.

There is actually something quite cathartic in externalising our worries and concerns. For some of these with the lowest totals, the process of naming and scoring will be sufficient for us to let them go, or there may be actions – requiring little time and effort – which may remove the worries from our minds and the list. The first part of addressing some of our worries is to enable a quick fix or forget them.

More mid-level concerns might need some specific actions to mitigate them. In looking at ways of mitigating various worries and concerns, it is often important to break them down into their constituent parts; to 'shrink the problem' (Heath and Heath, 2010) can move something from appearing overwhelming to being bite-size. An issue that might appear to be beyond your ability to influence may have a number of constituent elements that are more open to your direct control. Focus your efforts here.

It is important to keep in mind, as a leader, that you do not always have to be the doer. Across the organisation, there will be many competent, motivated and committed people who will be keen to step up and be a part of the potential solution. It is sensible and appropriate to give others a problem you are struggling with to see what solutions they can come up with. This is part of being a leader and part of creating new leaders.

Finally, there are the issues where the impact may be substantial and significant, longer term and affecting large parts or the whole organisation. These are the ones, if any, that should be keeping you awake at night. However, the process of risk assessment takes the worries and concerns from inside and moves them to a place where they can be viewed, interrogated and ultimately acted on. This gives a sense of empowerment, of being in control of events rather than at their mercy. I always found the former, no matter how challenging, preferential to the latter. Acting successfully to resolve an issue is a huge motivator.

Leaders must believe in their potential to influence and impact upon the world; life is not a preordained destiny. In viewing how people face various challenges, Freire (2017) noted that people were 'not limited to a single reaction pattern. They organize themselves, choose the best response, test themselves, act, and change in the very act of responding. They do all this consciously, as one uses a tool to deal with a problem.'

The opportunity to reflect – to think deeply and critically about an issue – and then act without unnecessary limitations, embodies empowerment. Leaders must see themselves as people who know and act. They must also enable others to do the same.

Be organised and systematic

Moving from introspective thought to effective action involves a leader keeping their focus on the main thing or things. Personal organisation is not just about calendars, diaries and to do lists. It is not simply about being in the right place at the right time. It is being in the right place all of the time. By this, I mean a leader needs to ensure their time and efforts are focused on the organisation's mission and the people who will make this mission a reality. While needing to keep an eye on operational matters, it is important to ensure sufficient time is given to more tactical and strategic issues. It is useful to think about the two timescales of a leader as now and eternity. This helps ensure the organisation's long-term mission is lived out in the daily reality experienced by staff, children and young people.

This requires a high level of self-discipline by leaders in order to maintain the organisation's priorities as their priorities. In *The 7 Habits of Highly Effective People* (2004) Stephen Covey writes about the personal victory of putting first things first. It is an approach to time management which is encapsulated in the phrase 'Organize and execute around priorities'. He looks at time management as interplay of the urgent and important.

A simple matrix identifies four quadrants: urgent and important (Q1); not urgent but important (Q2); not important but urgent (Q3); and neither urgent nor important (Q4). It is sometimes interesting to reflect on how much of each day you spend on the last two; unimportant meetings, emails, other people's priorities, interruptions or simple time wasters and trivia. Time spent in quadrant three (urgent but not important) and four (not important and not urgent) is almost all wasted. It is the dangerous illusion of busyness; too many people, working too hard, at too many things which are of limited importance. The number of 'priorities' are simply too great. Each priority has such limited time spent on it that it simply becomes another job to do and forget, before moving on to the next one. Nothing gets embedded, and little has any impact.

As a leader your challenge is to move the organisation forward as well as yourself. By choosing a few really important priorities, a few things which form a collective focus, you achieve so much more. The challenge of having real priorities is choosing the right ones to focus on at any particular time in the development and growth of an organisation. These important issues Covey (2004) placed in quadrant 1 (urgent and important) and quadrant 2 (important but not urgent). Quadrant 1 consists of pressing problems, occasional crises and short-deadline projects. These will be some of the things that kept you awake at night. However, many of the current list of greatest concerns and worries – important matters – did not need to reach the urgent stage. That is, by planning effectively around a few priorities you have time to act on them, if you choose to use your time to that end. Quadrant 2 (important but not urgent) is the space for planning and prevention, building relationships, and building your own and the organisation's capability. It is the space for the Basic of Introspection.

Over a number of years, I used a Q2 time management tool. There were a number of simple elements to it: identification of key priorities, acting on them in a timely manner and scheduling important actions or issues into specific time slots. This last point was ground-breaking for me. As a head of science, I took my twenty points to do list into a full five-period teaching day but then struggled to understand why I would end the day with the original points and a few more for good measure on the list. Accepting that time is limited and finite is a crucial part of the process of prioritising. Over the years, I came up with my own key practices and ways of working to help ensure that I was in the right place all of the time.

A couple of times each week, I would look forward to activities, events, and meetings coming up in the next three to four weeks. Some tasks have quite long lead in times, such as papers for directors' meetings. Others, like scripting a previously prepared presentation, I preferred to do no more than a day or two in advance. Some larger tasks need to be chunked down and completed over a few weeks, and each chunk would be scheduled in my diary. This involved working backwards from set deadlines, to make sure I had things done in good time, thus avoiding any last minute panics.

To help stay organised I only used (and still do) Google Calendar and Tasks, which are even slicker now the two are more integrated. I would suggest avoiding two calendars (digital and paper or work and home) or separate lists, everything is easier to manage if it is in one place. The key is finding something that works for you and remembering that life does not always go according to your plan. Wherever possible I would leave some time available each day to sort the mundane or the emergency, and if it was not required I would use it to get ahead. 'Leave perfection to God' was one of the most liberating statements I ever heard on a leadership course. I had spent far too long in my career trying to perfect various documents or activities. Not everything needs to be executed to near perfection; the time costs of perfecting things are not always worth the effort. When looking at an activity, event or set of documentation try to be clear about the standard required. You do not want to be or appear sloppy in presentation or thought but you do need to consider what is good enough. The time saved may be invested in other important aspects of your work or home life.

Maintaining this focus was a continual challenge. It was always far too easy to flick onto Twitter or the game app *2048* (my highest score of 286,536 took some practice). Emails can also become a distraction, continually flicking on and off the various inboxes to see what is happening or just trying to clear a backlog. Many organisations have now put in curfews. St. Mary's adopted a policy of no emails at weekends, between 5:00pm and 7:00am on workdays, and during holidays. If I wrote or answered emails outside of these times, I would always schedule the send to comply with the policy. Being organised and systematic helped free up a lot of time to focus on key Q2 activities. I shared my approach in *The five minute main thing plan* (#5MinMainThingPlan, http://wp.me/p3Gre8-HE) co-authored with Ross Morrison McGill.

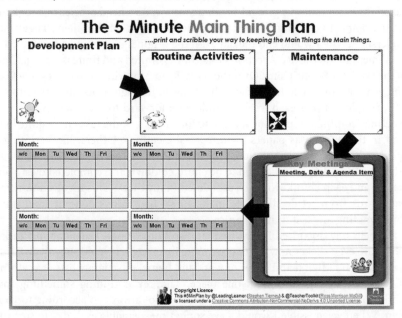

The plan was on one page. It pulled together all the improvements, priorities and activities that were scheduled to be completed in the term ahead. This timescale was important. Without looking at the various tasks and commitments months and weeks in advance there is a danger that workload builds up and important aspects of leaders' roles are not given enough time or forethought. This can lead to crisis points in a term where there are just not enough hours in the day to complete the work. As part of planning ahead, there is a need to be realistic about how much work can be reasonably done to a good standard, in the time available.

It is important to consider whether there are too many priorities. Are you setting yourself up to fail? Doing less but doing it better is preferable to starting hundreds of jobs and failing to complete them, or worse still making yourself ill. If you need to reduce the number of priorities so only the most important remain, this is a good time to do so.

Give consideration to the number, length and type of meetings in your diary. When you add up the total time and cost for everyone in a meeting it soon becomes apparent how precious meeting time is. On occasion, when calculating match funded contributions for a bid, it was common practice to add in the total cost of meeting time. An extended senior leadership meeting for an afternoon would be circa £2,500 to £3,000. Meetings involving twenty plus middle leaders would push up costs to between £7,500 to £10,000. These are real costs and meeting time needs to be understood as a precious resource. Hence the plan's suggestion to make sure you identify the dates for your key meetings for the term ahead, and assign the main agenda items from the development plan priorities, routine activities and maintenance issues previously identified. If a meeting has no substantive agenda it might be best to cancel it and allow people to use the time more productively. On occasion, I would not attend various meetings knowing that the minutes would give me all I really needed to know. Time is precious and cannot be spent twice.

The final thing was to schedule the 'main things' into the monthly planners. I would transfer across the key tasks and meetings to the specific dates and made sure I did not add any jobs or tasks on a date where I had a full teaching day or back-to-back meetings. On these days I was not going to get anything else done and it was no good pretending otherwise. I always tried to schedule time to prepare properly for a meetings, which included notifying colleagues, in good time, of any preparation they needed to do or papers they had to submit. Once you are into a good rhythm you will develop positive habits, such as having agendas and papers out a week in advance and follow up actions – with names and deadlines against each one – out within 48 hours.

The long list of jobs that need doing, many of which will never get done, haunts many leaders' waking hours. As the years went by, I became increasingly ruthless about what appeared in development plans and on my to do list. My mantra became; 'If it's not a nine or a ten out of ten, it's a no'. Saying 'no' to low priority jobs, meetings and tasks is a choice we need to exercise more often.

Ways of Knowing

Basic 3: Specialism

The importance of domain-specific knowledge and skills

An effective leader must be able to engage fully in the key discourse of their organisation. Through their coherent expert knowledge of the domain's complexity, they understand what is important and what is not. Focusing relentlessly on the former, leaders positively influence the thinking and actions of colleagues.

Summary

- Domain-specific knowledge includes: curriculum design; a deep understanding of the content to be taught; pedagogy to challenge pupils to think hard about the content; and assessment of and for learning. In addition, the creation of supportive environments to maximise pupils' opportunity to learn is required (Coe *et al.*, 2020).
- Within the expert teacher's mind each of the above areas of professional knowledge forms a comprehensive and connected schema. It is the increasing quantum – the number of different elements of specialist knowledge – and the interconnectedness within and between the various schemata that brings about greater expertise.
- This professional domain-specific knowledge is specialised, systemic and context-independent. The underpinning principles, concepts and theories may be transferred and used in a variety of appropriate contexts from Early Years to Higher Education.
- Within schools, domain-specific expertise changes at different levels within the organisation. Progressing from middle leadership to senior leadership requires different, additional domain-specific knowledge. An example of this is an understanding of the principles underpinning curriculum or assessment design.
- There is a danger when moving into senior leadership that middle leaders transfer domain-specific knowledge from their subject or phase directly into their whole school thinking and approach. Curriculum design, content, planning, teachers, pedagogy, learners and assessment vary by phase and subject.
- Leaders need to move beyond their own subject based domain thinking to a cross subject knowledge associated with broader underpinning principles.
- How senior leaders engage with phase and subject leaders is important. The concept and practising of subsidiarity are an important leadership consideration. On a practical level subsidiarity should be used to empower middle leaders and teachers as the primary professionals in their subject or phase.
- Whole school policy formation involves creating frameworks of agreed principles to provide direction and then enabling subject and phase leaders to use their domain-specific expertise to determine the more detailed operational ways of working.
- Due to the need to understand key domain-specific issues, schools should be led by well-informed leaders. That is, people who are grounded and rounded by their experiences of teaching. Leaders must have a profound understanding of the organisation's core business.
- Domain-specific knowledge and generic leadership knowledge are inter-related and form 'the what and the how' of leadership. Their relationship is entwined and nuanced rather than oppositional.

Specialism

In *A New Perspective for School Leadership,* Tom Rees (2020) suggested that there needs to be 'more focus on the specific educational work of school leaders and the expertise they need to do it well, and less focus on generic leadership concepts'. In exploring the key idea of domain-specific expertise he states 'There are two conflicting approaches we can take' referring to generic and domain-specific knowledge. Rees' thought-provoking piece, built around five key ideas influencing school leaders – complexity, domain-specific expertise, knowledge, persistent problems and context – was discussed and argued on Twitter, and the Klopp effect was mentioned often.

Liverpool Football Club were the force in English football during the 1970s and '80s as well as being successful in European competitions. By the 2019/20 season, Liverpool had not won the Premier League title (previously Division One) for thirty years. In March 2020, led by Jurgen Klopp, they were on the brink of their first league title for decades, twenty-five points ahead of their nearest rivals. They had won an unprecedented twenty-seven matches out of twenty-nine played with only two more wins required before they would be crowned champions. The equally unprecedented coronavirus halted their title charge. A thirty-year wait was agonisingly extended a few more months by the global pandemic. The team's success was attributed to the 'Klopp effect'.

Klopp's passion, commitment and knowledge of football were central to his and the team's success. He promoted *Gegenpressing* – a team's immediate attempt to win back possession high up the pitch, rather than falling back into a defensive formation – and coached players to implement it effectively. It is an example of domain-specific knowledge underpinning success. It is useful to contrast experiences where you have considerable domain knowledge to situations where you lack the specialist knowledge of others in the room. To what extent would you be able to effectively lead an organisation where your domain knowledge is limited?

While working at St. Mary's, I was invited to be the lay representative on board of the Blackpool Teaching Hospitals Local Education Providers. Approximately every other month I would attend a meeting alongside a large number of people who had profound knowledge and experience in the medical field. While a scientist, and interested in many things medical – my degree is in pharmacology – the content of the meetings was extremely specialised and well beyond my knowledge. The other attendees also had considerable experience of the organisation's functioning and hence how systems and processes operated.

Nearly all schools function five days a week, from Monday to Friday, with most staff working the same on-site hours and sharing the same holidays. This allows for the easy scheduling of lessons for pupils and professional development time for staff. Hospitals are quite different. Hospitals operate twenty-four hours a day and every day of the year. Medical staff, including trainees, work different days and different shifts. They also have no set holiday pattern. This created a complex and very different set of delivery challenges around professional development that were well outside of my experience. As such, I kept my contributions short, specific and to a general nature around programme planning and evaluation. They were often presented as a question, prompting others to consider and answer. This experience reinforced to me the importance of domain-specific knowledge.

Domain-specific knowledge

In an educational context, school leaders need domain-specific specialist knowledge. It is this Basic of Specialism that enables leaders to make well-informed decisions. To successfully lead a school, domain-specific knowledge is required relating to curriculum design, a deep understanding of the content to be taught and its sequencing, dependencies and common misconceptions, pedagogy to challenge pupils to think hard about the content taught, and assessment of and for learning. In addition, the creation of supportive environments that maximise pupils' opportunity to learn is needed (Coe et al, 2020).

Within the expert teacher's mind each of these areas of professional knowledge forms a comprehensive and connected schema. Knowledge from the different schemata is connected as teachers become increasingly expert. Underpinning patterns and ways of working are explicitly established and open to interrogation and revision. It is the increasing quantum – the number of different elements of specialist knowledge – and the interconnectedness of this knowledge that brings about greater expertise. This expertise is further enhanced by experience and professional development.

This professional domain-specific knowledge is analogous in many ways to Young's (2014) 'powerful knowledge' principle. Knowledge about curriculum design, content, pedagogy, assessment and the means to maximise the opportunity for pupils to learn is specialised and systemic. Within each area concepts are linked in an intentional way to create a coherent body of associated knowledge. The knowledge is well defined and has relatively fixed boundaries that enable a profession – in this case the teaching profession – to claim ownership of the knowledge. It is a key element in the profession's formation as a specialist community.

The knowledge is also context-independent. While some of the content may be phase- or subject-specific, the underpinning principles, concepts and theories may be transferred and used in a variety of appropriate contexts. In teaching these underpinning principles, concepts and theories need to be sensitively and expertly applied in contexts as varied as the Early Years and Foundation Stage, primary and secondary classrooms with different ages and subject requirements, university departments, and adult learning including continuous professional development.

While they believed that further research was required, Leithwood and colleagues (2019) determined a well-defined set of personal leadership resources – cognitive, social and psychological – that showed 'promise of explaining a high proportion of variation in the practices enacted by school leaders'. The authors proposed three elements; domain-specific knowledge, problem-solving and systems thinking, relating to the cognitive resources required by a leader. Central to these was domain-specific knowledge which enabled the problem-solving and systems thinking essential to successful school leadership. The domain-specific knowledge we use on a daily basis may well be taken for granted, but its importance cannot be understated when leading an educational organisation.

Curriculum entanglement

In the world of physics, quantum entanglement refers to the interaction of particles which are in such close proximity that the behaviour of each particle cannot be explained independently of the others. The term 'entanglement' neatly describes the dynamic interactivity of three entities (the content, the teacher and the learner) and three connecting processes (planning, pedagogy and assessment) in the teaching and learning process. Each can be considered as a distinct separate entity or process but to make sense of the whole they need to be considered together. This makes teaching truly and deeply complex.

Small changes in one or more of these six identifiable interconnected parts can lead to significant effects on, and consequences for, the other elements. An understanding of curriculum entanglement is part of the basic knowledge required by school leaders. This knowledge should be built on their own classroom experiences, and informed by theories and evidence.

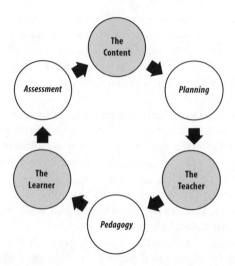

Heinrich Bauersfeld (1979) linked three of these interdependent and internally dynamic structures: the structure of the content or subject to be learnt (matter meant); the structure of the instruction or pedagogy (matter taught) and the cognitive structure developed by the pupils (matter learnt). While the paper was written about the mathematics curriculum, it is applicable across a range of subjects and age ranges. Educators in England may be more familiar with the alternative terms used in Ofsted's *Education Inspection Framework* (2019); curriculum intent, implementation and impact. The latter term was changed from Bauersfeld's original term, 'enacted', and it is important to see impact in terms of the matter learnt rather than examination outcomes. This is because assessments form a critical part of the teaching process particularly when the outcome remains in a disaggregated state. That is, rather than aggregating a pupil's answers into an overall grade or mark, the teacher is aware of what the pupil does or does not know, or can or cannot do.

When speaking to teachers, particularly those new to the profession, I describe the challenge as 'getting the pictures in your heads into the pupils' heads'. There is a need therefore to ensure these pictures (or more correctly schemata) in the teacher's head are explicit and secure, before they can be taught to the pupils. In this respect the detailed planning of learning over a whole unit of work is a crucial prerequisite to planning lessons. When the former is done well, it makes sense to keep lesson planning more minimal and fluid, so teachers are able to respond to the actual flow of learning in the classroom. Too often lesson plans are produced in detail and adhered to in spite of pupils' actual rate of learning.

When first teaching science, I was demonstrating the effect of heat on the expansions of a metal. It was a simple ball and hoop experiment; when cool, the metal ball just fits through a hoop, but after being heated it no longer does. Pupils were then asked to offer suggestions as to why this might be so, but I was not fully prepared for their explanations. More than half the class suggested that the particles had got bigger. Scientifically, we explain the metal ball's expansion due to the particles moving further apart. However, the pupils' theory of the particles getting bigger made perfect sense. Being prepared to respond to this suggestion – preparing pupils for the fact that there might be two different suggestions – and having an appropriate explanation as to why scientists believe the particles move further apart during expansion, would have been of great assistance. It was a moment where I needed to go off-piste, leaving the comfort of the lesson plan and working in the messy reality that is classroom learning.

Alongside building positive relationships and motivating pupils to work hard, good teachers have the knack of building pupils' understanding over time in a systematic way. Their approach is rooted in experience and informed by evidence and associated theories of teaching and learning. Teachers do not suddenly become experts. Their expertise starts with an understanding of how we learn and the planning of what must be learnt, and progresses through the use of effective pedagogy to an assessment of what has been learnt.

What pupils already know or think they know needs to be taken into account. The best teachers seem to be able to get into the heads of their pupils to see the schemata in formation. They also then respond appropriately, tailoring the learning to that of their pupils. The challenge for senior leaders is converting their knowledge and practice of teaching a subject or phase into an understanding of the principles of effective practice that may be more generally applied across the curriculum. This more principle-based level of understanding is the specialist knowledge required by leaders.

The SOLO taxonomy (Structure of the Observed Learning Outcome)

Assessments enable us to draw inferences. Stripping assessment back, the everyday primary need for teachers is to connect what has been taught – the 'matter meant' – to the 'matter learnt' by pupils. To what extent has the content I have taught and the purpose behind teaching it been assimilated by pupils? Assessment sits at this pivotal point between teaching and learning. This was the basis of the SOLO (Structure of the Observed Learning Outcome) taxonomy proposed by Biggs and Collis (1982). By examining the structure of the observed learning outcome (SOLO) teachers are able to gain an insight into 'what might or might not be happening in the learner's mind' (Wiliam, 2014). These insights may include both what pupils appear to know and what gaps or misconnections between various elements of content they currently have.

The SOLO taxonomy was used to analyse the overall quality of pupils' work in terms of its complexity, and a common pattern emerged as work progressed from low quality to the highest quality. At the lower end, work showed that pupils had not understood, retained or were able to retrieve what had been taught. This was termed pre-structural. Some pupils were able to demonstrate limited evidence of knowledge, with one relevant aspect of what had been taught (uni-structural) contained within their answer. This progressed to pupils who were able to communicate their increasing knowledge about what had been taught by identifying a number of relevant aspects in their response (multi-structural). Both uni-structural and multi-structural responses provide evidence of surface knowledge; a necessary precursor to deeper understanding. This then progressed to a deeper understanding involving knowledge at a relational level and the extended abstract as greater connectivity between the elements was established. The highest quality work consisted of a greater number of elements (facts, ideas, concepts, laws) and a greater number of connections between them. This connectivity is sometimes referred to as interactivity.

Imagine pupils were asked to respond to a question about the causes of the First World War. At a uni-structural level they might write about the assassination of Archduke Franz Ferdinand and his wife by a Serbian nationalist in June 1914. At a multi-structural level, in addition to the assassination they could include in their answer details about Austria's declaration of war on Serbia and how other countries became involved as allies on either side. What would be lacking is a wider perspective and a linking of the events to the underlying historical causes.

As pupils' responses start to identify, link and explain the historical causes: mutual defence alliances countries had formed over time; the growth of European imperialism in the quest to acquire a greater share of resources available in Africa and parts of Asia, which led to a number of smaller confrontations; militarism through the increasing influence of the military on politics and a growth of the size of armies and navies in some countries; and nationalism, with various countries trying to prove their dominance and power. The pupil is now operating at a relational level and is showing a deep understanding (knowledge) of the causes of the First World War.

At the final level of the taxonomy, the extended abstract, the pupil would be able to use the relational thinking described above to show how Europe had been a powder keg for a century, and that the First World War had been an accident waiting to happen. Generalising to show how conflicts, while having a trigger, are caused by deeper geo-political, economic and social reasons would represent the highest quality response.

These insights into what cognitive structures a pupil may have developed as a consequence of teaching are invaluable. Interestingly, the SOLO Taxonomy is not only of value as an assessment tool but can be used within planning. By considering the different elements, interactions and dependencies of a set body of knowledge, thought may be given to how the knowledge may be sequenced and a certain teaching order determined. Coe and colleagues (2020) identified 'four priorities for teachers who want to help their student learn more'. The first priority was that teachers must understand 'the content they are teaching and how it is learnt'. Key aspects identified as part of this priority, were teachers having deep and fluent knowledge and flexible understanding of the content, knowledge of the requirements of curriculum sequencing and dependencies, and knowledge of common student strategies, misconceptions and sticking points.

By using planning and assessment as an evaluative process – linking what is taught with what pupils learn – planning, pedagogy and ultimately learning may all be improved.

Linking to cognitive load theory

As our professional knowledge and teaching experience increase, we can start to appreciate the complexity of various entangled elements. This enables us to make links and develop underlying principles to inform our practice.

There is a need to understand the importance of both managing cognitive load by reducing or limiting the number of elements taught at any one time, and carefully sequencing the information to connect it to prior learning. One of the five critically important compound (underpinning) effects identified in *Cognitive Load Theory* (Sweller *et al.*, 2019) is termed the element interactivity effect. This effect compares low and high element interactivity; the greater the number of elements and connections between them, the higher the interactivity. Linking back to the SOLO taxonomy, learning gains are associated with an increasing knowledge of a number of the elements (uni- to multi-structural) and then connecting the elements together (relational). These are clearly two mutually reinforcing ideas.

However, complexity does not just depend on the content, it also depends on the relative expertise of the learner. What is complex to a novice is readily understandable to an expert, due to expert learners already possessing complex schemata in their long-term memory which they can readily transfer into their working memory. Teaching practices and materials designed for novices contain information already known by experts, unnecessarily adding to the more expert learner's cognitive load. This led to what cognitive load theory termed the expertise reversal effect, another one of its compound effects. Hence, with increasing expertise, many of the strategies proposed for novice learners are less effective or even detrimental to experts. As pupils increase their knowledge, teachers need to change their pedagogy.

This links to a third compound effect in cognitive load theory, termed the guidance fading effect, which is closely related to the two compound effects above. Tom Sherrington (2019) grouped together three of Rosenshine's principles – guided practice, high success rate and independent practice – into what he termed stages of practice. One of the aims of our teaching is to help pupils become increasingly independent as learners, which could be expressed as reducing or fading guidance. One approach to increasing independence is carefully withdrawing the support and scaffolds used to assist learning. Another is to challenge pupils with more complex tasks including problem solving, analysis and synthesis of ideas, and creating links between associated concepts. Element interactivity, expertise reversal and guidance fading are, in essence, another lens through which to view the entanglement of content, learner and pedagogy.

As teachers, when our domain knowledge increases, we develop a greater quantum of and connectivity between associated concepts, and through experience we determine how these may be best enacted in the classroom; over time we evaluate and refine our practice. Cognitive load theory builds upon long established findings from cognitive science about the interaction of working memory and long-term memory. Sweller and colleagues' (2019) concern that this interaction 'has had a limited impact on the field of instructional design with most instructional design recommendations proceeding as though working memory and long-term memory did not exist' is beginning to be addressed. Interest in effective approaches from findings in cognitive science, including retrieval practice and distributed or spaced learning, is beginning to be more prevalent.

Due to the need to understand key domain issues such as curriculum entanglement, I would always want to see schools led by well-informed headteachers. That is, people who are grounded and rounded by their experiences of teaching. I am less concerned about whether they actually continue to teach while being a headteacher, as in part that will be determined by context, conditions and pressures on time. What is non-negotiable is the need for the leader of a school to have a profound understanding of the organisation's core business. The business of curriculum design, a deep understanding of the content to be taught, pedagogy to challenge pupils to think hard, and assessment of and for learning. This is the specialist knowledge which enables the school leader to engage knowledgeably in the key discourse of the organisation.

The changing domain

Within schools, the domain-specific knowledge required at different levels within the organisation changes. Progressing from middle leadership – with responsibilities for a phase or subject – to senior leadership requires additional domain-specific knowledge, whereas changes from classroom to middle leadership are more subtle.

Moving to Head of Science, via responsibility for chemistry and then also biology, I remained rooted in the practice of teaching science. Middle leadership challenged me to take into account different effective practices of often older and more experienced science teachers while seeking to develop a cohesive view of the teaching of science. My knowledge of science and my increasing experience of teaching it was the foundation of many discussions; pedagogical content knowledge is front and centre of the classroom teacher's and subject leader's domain knowledge.

However, there is a danger when moving into senior leadership that you transfer this domain-specific knowledge – from your subject or phase – directly into your whole school thinking and approach. Consider curriculum design, content, pedagogy or assessment from the perspective of an Early Years Foundation Stage teacher compared to a Key Stage 2 colleague. Early years has elements of domain-specific knowledge that are at a phase level rather than at a school level. If a senior leader was seeking to transfer the practices of early years, rather than underpinning principles, to the increasingly more subject-based upper primary curriculum, it would undoubtedly lead to problems. The same is true when upper primary practice is inappropriately transferred into early years.

For subject leaders at a secondary or sixth form level, there needs to be an understanding that the subject-based domain thinking – in English, mathematics, science, religious education, art, drama, design technology, history, geography, modern foreign languages, music, and physical education – needs to be advanced to consider broader underpinning principles. Grasping this took me years and led to hours of frustration for both myself and the subject leaders. I could not understand why my detailed whole school one size fits all curriculum, teaching and learning, assessment or marking policies could not be applied to their subjects. It was because my science subject domain differed to theirs.

When teaching science at a school level, substantive knowledge is pretty much fixed and not open to debate. It must be learnt by pupils and disciplinary approaches are used to reinforce the substantive knowledge. Many science teachers will know the feeling of experimental results – both demonstrations and class experiments – having to be ignored as they failed to support the prevailing orthodoxy. This is very different to the teaching of other subjects where disciplinary approaches are central to questioning in art, history and English literature. Substantive knowledge may be more limited in some subjects, and inferences open to greater questioning. This affects the source, style, scope and detail of policies. School leaders should seek to create policies consisting of frameworks of agreed principles to provide a sense of direction and cohesion. These policies must then enable subject and phase leaders to use their domain-specific expertise to determine the more detailed operational ways of working.

How senior leaders engage with phase and subject leaders is important. To what extent does the senior leader wish to be the expert in each subject or phase domain and to what extent do they wish to promote the expertise of the subject or phase leader? It is worth noting the empirical evidence supporting the premise that, 'School Leadership can have an especially positive influence on school and student outcomes when it is distributed' (Leithwood *et al.*, 2019). The concept and practising of subsidiarity are an important leadership consideration. On a practical level subsidiarity should be used to empower middle leaders and teachers as the primary professionals in their subject or phase.

From specific practice to underpinning principles

The establishment of principles by which to view the curriculum, pedagogy and assessment allows leaders to look at these complex areas from different perspectives. Binary viewpoints and the proposal of simple solutions belie the complexity of these issues. There are often trade-offs that need to be accepted, for example making assessment more manageable may have an impact on the relative reliability of data, and as such any inferences drawn have to be more tentative in nature. Or looking at the impact of a more vertically integrated curriculum on a curriculum's coherence. Part of making these decisions is being able to see and understand the underpinning principles and the implications of different choices.

Leaders need to be able to enact the organisation's purpose through its key components; vision, curriculum, pastoral care and support, behaviour system and the professional development offered to staff. While purpose is one influence on these components, there are also political and societal influences which must be taken into account. Without a leaders' principle-led understanding of the complexities involved, these latter influences may subvert an organisation's purpose.

Born in the early 1960s, I am part of a generation which has seen significant and substantial improvements in equality legislation. Attending a new comprehensive school in the 1970s, the lower secondary curriculum would now appear to be from the dark ages. As a boy in a higher set, I did woodwork and metalwork for one term each over the three years. Most of my time in these lessons was spent in technical drawing, whereas boys from lower sets spent their time working with tools in metalwork and woodwork, and the girls did cooking and needlework. The next decade saw considerable curriculum change. By the late 1980s and 1990s, when I taught science, ensuring more girls studied STEM (Science, Technology, Engineering and Mathematics) subjects post-16 was a key objective. Central to these changes was an underpinning focus on the empowerment of groups of young people who had previously been disadvantaged or discriminated against. There was a move away from preparation for work, which had previously been hugely stereotyped, towards directing greater numbers of young people towards a university education.

There has also been a development of youth culture since the 1960s. Adolescence formed a distinct separate identity to childhood and adulthood. Young people asserted their right to have a voice and choice about fashion, music and leisure. Pupil voice and curriculum choice, in terms of the options post-14, became part of education. Attending a secondary school in the 1970s, my O-level choices were available via four different option blocks with a small prescribed core curriculum. This level of choice is rarely seen in schools today. In part, this is a politically driven decision based around a significantly extended core curriculum based on a set of E-Bacc subjects.

This political influence is part of a substantially greater focus on cultural transmission as the predominant philosophy within the purpose of education. Associated with the philosophy of transmission has been the promotion of a zero tolerance approach to behaviour, with rules about silence in corridors and the mooting of a statutory mobile phone ban in schools. This impacts further on a young person's voice and choice, and while some in education applaud the clear focus, others decry the narrowing of the purpose to education. I consider the benefit of the current emphasis to be an enhanced understanding of how to ensure high quality transmission, particularly at a subject level. This is a good thing but also an insufficient one. In the coming years, as politicians change, schools may be faced with a fresh drive for a more work-orientated curriculum or focus on empowerment or engagement with the community. School leaders need to be able to ride out various political biases with a strong principle-focused sense of purpose.

From curriculum entanglement to curriculum design

All teachers must be well versed in the curriculum entanglement relating to the content, the teacher and the learner; and planning, pedagogy and assessment. This is part of the specialist knowledge senior leaders require but it is not enough; senior leaders need to understand the curriculum at a subject or phase level and additionally at a whole school level. Usefully, Wiliam (2013) produced a series of seven curriculum design principles which may be used to help shape thinking, guide discussions between senior and middle leaders, and influence decisions about the curriculum overall. Four of the seven principles proposed are below. They have quite specific and specialist meaning.

Rigorous	Seeks to develop intra-disciplinary habits of mind; the subject matter is taught in a way that is faithful to its discipline.
Vertically integrated	Focuses on progression by carefully sequencing knowledge; provides clarity about what 'getting better' at the subject means.
Appropriate	Seeks to avoid making unreasonable demands by matching the level of challenge to a pupil's current level of maturity/knowledge.
Focused	Looks to keep the curriculum manageable by teaching the most important knowledge; identifies the big ideas or key concepts within a subject.

When considering the principles of rigour, vertical integration and appropriateness, it is reasonable to assume that middle leaders' expert subject or phase knowledge would allow them to take a lead on these matters. For senior leaders, the key is to provide time for the training – at a departmental or phase level – so these matters can be fully considered. The issue of sufficient time cannot be understated.

Too often the expectations of teachers and middle leaders with respect to curriculum development are unrealistic. Teachers must be personally involved in curriculum development, which should be viewed as a key aspect of professional development (Howson, 1979). The opportunity to discuss and debate the most important content for pupils to master, key misconceptions that are likely to be encountered, the sequencing of the curriculum and dependencies, and effective pedagogy, tasks and assessments, provides valuable opportunities for an integrated approach to curriculum and professional development. Curriculum development is inexorable; it must be viewed as the gradual cumulative process it undoubtedly is.

One area where I believe senior leaders may operate as critical friends is that of focus. The most challenging curriculum questions – from the perspective of content – always centre around what should be left out. In an uncompromising statement, Dylan Wiliam (Lough, 2020) described the teaching of a content-heavy curriculum as 'immoral' because 'it leaves the majority of pupils behind'. His concern was that curriculum developers tend to overfill the curriculum with far too much content for most pupils to assimilate. It is critical that the curriculum's content is learnt, not just encountered at an increasingly frenetic pace.

If the curriculum has reached what Kingsnorth (2019) refers to as the Goldilocks Plateau – 'that point beyond which not everyone can master all of the content' – the issue of mastering the content is one of having sufficient time per objective or threshold concept. Kingsnorth suggests looking at the curriculum in terms of: the level of difficulty or challenge; the number of objectives or amount of content; and the amount of time available to teach each objective. A conversation as to whether the planned curriculum has just the right amount of content, at just the right level of challenge, for the majority of pupils, given the time available, is a useful one for senior and middle leaders to engage in.

However, three of the principles proposed by Wiliam (2013) need to be determined at a senior level, often with the involvement of governors. These principles cannot be considered at a purely subject or phase level.

Balanced	Promotes intellectual, moral, spiritual, aesthetic, creative, emotional and physical development as equally important.
Relevant	Seeks to connect the valued outcomes of a curriculum to the pupils being taught it; provides opportunities for pupils to make informed choices.
Coherent	Makes explicit connections and links between the different subjects and experiences encountered.

The E-Bacc, at Key Stage 4, has produced a broad but largely unbalanced curriculum for many pupils. It promotes the intellectual but leaves many of the other aspects of a balanced curriculum on the periphery, and it may also lack relevance, in turn undermining personal empowerment. Ensuring a balanced curriculum is a key decision for senior leaders, as is the point at which relevance becomes a primary driver of the curriculum. Relevance allows a pupil to make informed decisions about what their curriculum should look like. To what extent and at what age should a young person be able to make an informed choice about which aspects of their curriculum they will study or how they wish to study and learn? This could involve a young person deciding to pursue a curriculum giving a greater emphasis to vocational programmes, the arts (choosing to study art, drama and music) or STEM subjects. These choices will have an impact on the balance of their curriculum.

The issue of developing a coherent curriculum has significant implications for vertical integration. While it is not quite an 'either or' choice, the connecting of knowledge from different subjects so it may be taught as part of a thematic curriculum will have implications for the sequencing of the curriculum within a subject and *vice versa*. In the end the curriculum design principles create a series of questions that leaders must answer. I discuss these issues in greater detail in *Educating with Purpose*, which examines how the curriculum must be aligned with purpose.

Assessment

As a senior leader, I was able to take significant domain knowledge about assessment in science into the whole school issues I had responsibility for. In science, primarily assessing substantive knowledge through the use of multiple-choice questions, short answers and labelling of diagrams allowed large areas of the curriculum to be assessed in a reasonably short period of time. The established facts, concepts and laws taught and assessed in primary and secondary science are not open to debate or interpretation, so the marking of these questions was relatively quick and simple.

Assessment in other subjects, for example English literature, is substantially and significantly different. This is due in part to the different balance between substantive and disciplinary knowledge within the subject, and the nature of the extended written responses provided by pupils, which lead to different assessment requirements. This is the point at which senior leaders need to defer the details of assessment to the subject or phase leader. The broad principles within an assessment policy need to cover important aspects of assessment; the following five principles for summative assessment were proposed by Dylan Wiliam at a symposium in Manchester in 2013:

- Trusted (do stakeholders have faith in the outcomes?)
- Distributed (so that evidence collection is not undertaken entirely at the end)
- Synoptic (so that learning has to accumulate)
- Extensive (so that all important aspects are covered)
- Manageable (so that costs are proportionate to benefits).

The final one remains a key issue in many schools. For most of my time teaching and leading schools, teachers were over-marking and under-planning. Further, too little of the marking was for the benefit of the pupils or the teacher. Too much was about satisfying the insatiable accountability regime. The increased use of data linked to classroom and school-based assessments, enabled through the use of complex management information systems, led to a whole series of undesirable practices being employed in schools. Two key assessment concepts needed to be more fully understood by school leaders and teachers, namely validity and reliability. These affect the extent to which key stakeholders can have faith in the outcomes and inferences being made.

Many assessments in schools are of the moment in nature. They need an immediate interpretation by a teacher or pupils and on many occasions elicit a potentially unplanned for response. This can require a teacher to rethink their plan for the lesson to take account of what pupils do or don't know, or for pupils to rethink their incomplete or incorrect answers. The assessment information is low stakes, largely ephemeral in nature and only ever known to the teacher and pupils, and it should stay that way; 'assessment should be the servant, not the master, of the learning' (Wiliam, 2014). Unfortunately, the accountability system outside the school and the monitoring and audit system within it sought to capture it as quasi-evidence of pupil progress or how effectively teachers were performing their role. The conclusions drawn lacked validity.

Validity is a concept associated with the inferences or conclusions being drawn from assessments. The validity of any particular inference or conclusion is affected by the reliability of the assessment – the extent to which the assessment yields consistent data – which in turn is influenced by two main elements. The first is that the assessment is too small (termed construct under-representation) and does not assess important elements that it should. A short test on a year's work is unlikely to cover all the important content of the programme and for too many pupils there will be an element of luck whether they have learnt and revised the specific limited content on the test. The second is that the assessment is too big (termed construct-irrelevance variation) and contains elements that are not relevant to the conclusions the assessor wishes to draw. This might include a very high reading age for a science test or variations between what markers will accept as right or wrong answers. A lack of understanding about the limitations of the assessment data being collected led school leaders to make poor decisions.

In the busyness of school life, teachers and leaders sometimes want simple solutions to complex problems. The desire to implement something, on occasion anything, to try to drive improvement without understanding the deeper connections between key elements becomes the overriding driver. As the holistic thinking disappears, the bright spots remain but their rich connectivity and interactivity are lost. The school is left with a series of seemingly silver coated bullets rather than the rich understanding required to shape and direct classroom practice. In the absence of deep domain-specific knowledge, school leaders adopt shallow practices too quickly; rapidly abandoning them before moving on to next new and best thing proposed.

Domain-specific knowledge is critically important to effective school leadership, but it is not enough on its own. Specialist knowledge needs to be utilised alongside strategic knowledge, and leaders are often required to make informed decisions based on information across a range of discrete but connected domains. I do not consider domain-specific knowledge and more generic leadership knowledge to be in conflict, they are inter-related and form the what and the how of leadership. Their relationship is entwined and nuanced rather than oppositional, I would liken it to the operating systems and application software that enable our mobile phones and computers to work. The application software is analogous to the specificity of the domain knowledge. The more generic operating system, on which the application software performs its function, forms a base from which different software (domains) may effectively function.

Basic 4: Strategy

The importance of generic leadership knowledge and skills

An effective leader has a holistic understanding of the organisation and the external environment. They have an enhanced knowledge of and experience across a range of related and interacting domains. This enables them to focus and align the work on the organisation's key strategic priorities, bringing coherence and direction to the organisation's work.

Summary

- Strategy adds knowledge of the 'know-how' to the 'know what' of domain-specific knowledge.
- Three generic domains of practice required by leaders across very different organisations are: setting direction; building relationships and developing people; and supporting desired practices (Leithwood *et al.*, 2019).
- Strategy forms part of a leader's decision making framework. It involves knowledge of how best to act in order to focus, align and execute work on the organisation's key priorities.
- Specialism and strategy combine to allow consideration of five aspects associated with organisational improvement and development: content, sequencing, timescales, tactics and responsiveness.
- Two key aspects of strategy are enhanced knowledge of a wide range of related domains and a set of mental models underpinning important leadership behaviours.
- The balance between the strategic and domain-specific knowledge required depends upon a number of factors. As the size of the organisation increases both strategic and domain knowledge need to be more balanced.
- Four styles of leadership – visionary, coaching, affiliative and democratic – create a resonance or positive emotions which boost individual and organisational performance. Two further styles – pacesetting and commanding – have very specific uses and must be used with care (Goleman *et al.*, 2002).
- Repeating patterns of change are based upon the extent to which the change has a clear, defined end point or not and whether the means of change is predetermined by the leader or delegated to the group to decide.
- A key role of governance is providing strategic direction to the organisation. It is important to engage the governing body and senior leaders in joint development planning. This helps ensure change is a process over time rather than an event.
- Big strategic moves link together: mission – why we exist; values – what we believe in and how we will behave; and vision – what we want to be. This involves reconciling 'ends to means through strategic intent' (Hamel and Prahalad, 1989). Strategic intent involves a sense of direction, discovery and destiny.
- In deep partnership working, the issue of who leads is often the elephant in the room. Leaders may feel more comfortable in shallow partnerships that allow maximum autonomy.

Strategy

School leaders need profound domain-specific knowledge relating to the curriculum, substantive and disciplinary knowledge and its organisation, pedagogy, and a range of factors which influence learning and the learner. Domain-specific knowledge is critically important but alone is insufficient. School leaders are required to bring alive these domain-specific elements within their organisation. In addition to improving the instructional programme (domain-specific), Leithwood and colleagues (2019) identified three further domains of practice which 'almost all successful leaders draw on': setting direction (relating to vision and performance); building relationships and developing people; and supporting desired practices (distributing leadership and a collaborative culture within the organisation and with partners). These three final domains of practice are the generic leadership knowledge and skills required by leaders across very different organisations, they are part of a strategic approach to leadership.

Knowing how best to act in order to focus, align and execute work on the organisation's key priorities is at the heart of the Basic of Strategy. Strategic knowledge forms part of the decision making framework (Bungay, 2019) used by leaders. Strategy adds knowledge of 'know-how' to the 'know what' of specialist domain-specific knowledge. Both are required for effective leadership, and must help produce an alignment and coherence between an organisation's purpose and its enactment. Strategic decision making is the linchpin of the process.

These two different 'ways of knowing' – specialism and strategy – enable leaders to look holistically at the development and improvement of the organisation through consideration of:

- Content – what are the key elements of the organisation that need to be improved or developed?
- Sequence – in what order should we address these various elements? Are there any dependencies? Is anything urgent?

- Timescales – how long do we think each element may take to effectively plan, implement and embed? How can we build the necessary capacity to ensure the job gets done?
- Tactics – how can we best achieve our desired outcomes? How will we establish and embed new practices as norms within our way of working?
- Responsiveness – when and how will we review our plans in order to respond to emerging data of impact (feedback loops) or previously unknown or unforeseen events? Who do we need to involve?

Developing priorities and development planning

Most development planning follows a deliberate approach to strategy formulation; it is a master plan using broad brush strokes to give a shared focus to the organisation's work. The formal planning is based on the assumptions that leaders can predict the future state with sufficient accuracy, that the organisation can be internally structured to meet the new requirements and that the change will occur within structured parameters (Rose and Cray, 2010).

Below is the strategic overview of the plan developed for The Blessed Edward Bamber Catholic Multi-Academy Trust. It is for the period from September 2015 to August 2020 and contained broadly based objectives which helped provide a shared focus and sense of direction. Each objective involved a significant piece of work, and mindful of the capacity within the schools, various start points for each of the objectives were agreed, with some being years down the line. Objectives that we had not already been working on had a year-long development stage, which was a major change from previous practice which had tended towards implement first, think later.

New Objectives		Academic Years				
		2015/16	2016/17	2017/18	2018/19	2019/20
1	Implement a challenging spiral Mathematics & Numeracy Curriculum from Key Stage 1 to 5	Implement	Implement	Embed		
2	Develop & Implement a challenging spiral English & Literacy Curriculum from Key Stage 1 to 5	Develop	Implement	Implement	Embed	
3	Develop & Implement a challenging spiral Religious Education Curriculum from Key Stage 1 to 5		Develop	Implement	Implement	Embed
4	Develop & Implement a challenging spiral Science Curriculum from Key Stage 1 to 5			Develop	Implement	Implement

#	Objective					
5	Teaching Approach directed towards challenging next stage ready assessments and associated closing the gap processes	Implement	Implement	Embed		
6	Develop & Implement a stage appropriate professional development curriculum for teachers		Implement	Implement	Embed	
7	Develop and share an expertise in primary/ secondary transition in core subjects as part of an external CPD offer		Develop	Implement	Implement	Embed
8	Implement a Quality Assurance Programme across the Trust with external validation/ peer review	Implement	Embed			
9	Develop & Implement a Healthy Minds, Healthy Mindset Strategy to address mental health and resilience barriers to achievement	Develop	Implement	Implement	Implement	Embed
10	Develop & Implement a recruitment & retention strategy based on a positive ethos, workload reform, professional development and enhanced opportunities for staff	Develop	Implement	Embed		

By simply reading the objectives it is obvious the development plan belongs to a school or educational organisation, and substantial specialist knowledge was required to determine the content. The content, sequencing and timescales were all derived from leaders' specialist understanding of education, with the whole being influenced by national policy decisions. The primacy given to English, literacy, mathematics and numeracy was, in part, a response to a new Primary National Curriculum being introduced.

Despite five different Secretaries of State for Education during the plan's lifetime – Gove, Morgan, Greening, Hinds and Williamson – the written plan remained largely intact with limited changes. Over the five-year period, objective three was adapted, objective seven changed, and an eleventh objective was added. By the 2019/20 academic year these read:

3. Develop and implement a challenging spiral religious education and HRSE, history and geography curriculum from EYFS to post-16.
7. Develop St. Mary's Catholic Academy as a research school for the Blackpool Opportunity Area.
11. Implement an effective strategy to increase the number of post-16 students in St. Mary's sixth form.

Each strategic objective had four or five key actions associated with it which were written, implemented and monitored on an annual basis. This allowed some variation within the strategic framework from what was originally conceived. Variations included redirecting the English and Literacy objective to primarily focus on reading. Another variation involved implementing some significant cross-phase collaboration to provide subject expertise and professional development while the primary schools' religious education and science schemes of learning were developed. Other changes included amending timescales, as it always took longer to develop, implement and embed each objective than initially thought. Rather than stretch the available capacity we would delay an objective by twelve months to ensure effective implementation and embedding of the ones we were working on. These are all examples of the responsiveness that may be required as long-term plans are implemented.

While the content and sequencing of a school's development plan rely largely on specialist educational domain-specific knowledge, strategic knowledge is required to build the capacity needed to ensure the plan is effectively implemented. More often than not, teachers and leaders find a lack of time to be the main obstacle to improvement work. The capacity available will impact upon the timescales required to successfully implement a particular objective. On a number of occasions, we increased the time available for a particular objective through permanent or fixed term appointments. Understanding the financial and human resources implications of staffing decisions is critical if schools are not to end up with budget deficits, and this knowledge is even more vital in the austere times we live in.

Enhanced knowledge and mental models
Strategy requires enhanced knowledge of a wide range of related domains and a set of mental models underpinning important leadership behaviours. These help leaders make informed decisions about the most effective tactics to be used in a particular situation or context. Enhanced knowledge may be categorised as that beyond the everyday knowledge of an intelligent person but not as substantive as that of an expert in the particular domain.

As a school leader, I would require enhanced knowledge of finance, human resources, data, premises, health and safety, risk assessment, project management and the development of processes and systems. In addition, I would need knowledge of various legal aspects relating to education and employment. Understanding the local and macro social and political environments in which you lead also helps support good decision making. The list is daunting, and it is no wonder many senior leaders are put off headship. The range of enhanced knowledge may be summarised by the acronym PESTLE: Political, Economic, Social, Technological, Legal and Environmental.

It is inefficient and potentially damaging to revert to an expert on every occasion that enhanced strategic knowledge is required. It is akin to suggesting domain knowledge is no longer required as we now have Google. The ability to think as a school leader requires both domain and strategic knowledge to be readily available in long-term memory. There are times when expert advice and input will be required, and leaders may still need to balance sometimes contradictory advice and the assessed risks of action or inaction. This is the thinking associated with the tactics of how to best achieve the desired outcomes in order to establish and embed new practices as norms into the organisation's way of working.

Middle leadership – and too often senior leadership – in schools do not prepare people well for the range and level of knowledge they are likely to require. Early in my headship I was too reliant on the knowledge of experts in various fields. A number of these experts were employees, some were contracted to work with the organisation through service level agreements and others were engaged on a more flexible consultancy basis. I sought to learn quickly, and over time I gained greater expertise through experience and other forms of professional development. I also soon found out which school leader might be best to phone when I encountered a particular problem.

Without this enhanced level of knowledge across a range of domains it is too easy to have the wool pulled over your eyes, miss strategic opportunities to further the organisation's mission or miss the significance of a particular announcement, set of data or change in regulations. The ability to connect a variety of information brings coherence, making sense of how the different parts fit and interact, and is the key to strategic work. As a leader you can delegate the tasks, but you cannot delegate the understanding. With greater understanding comes an enhanced awareness of what to delegate and to whom.

The balance between the generic strategic and domain-specific knowledge required depends upon a number of factors. In smaller organisations the more generic leadership work may be less of a priority as structures, systems and processes can be replaced by a more dialogical approach. Communication systems can be simpler and more ephemeral in nature. As an organisation establishes or grows both generic and domain knowledge need to be more balanced. The increased size and stability of the organisation need to be recognised in structures, systems, processes and communication. Leading a small primary school is very different to leading a multi-academy trust consisting of twenty or thirty schools.

In larger organisations, the different domain-specific knowledge required often sits across multiple teams, such as education, human resources, finance, marketing, and research and development. All these teams have different domain-specific knowledge. A leader is required to ensure the whole is greater than the sum of the parts; in essence, they are required to create coherence and synergies. Alongside this enhanced multi-domain knowledge is the more tacit knowledge possessed by a leader. I would describe this as mental models about leadership. These determine how leaders behave; the mental models create an underlying operating system from which a leader's tactical approach emanates.

With greater experience, leaders intuitively view change from a number of perspectives: whether means and endpoints are fixed or open to choice; whether the focus is primarily task or people orientated or a balance of both; and how best to approach the work at each juncture. These mental models allow leaders to behave in a context appropriate manner when managing people to ensure important work is completed efficiently and to a high standard.

Styles of leadership and patterns of change

Among the various mental models of leadership which influenced how I led, were the six leadership styles proposed by Goleman and colleagues (2002). The authors' premise was that 'No matter what leaders set out to do … their success depends on how they do it.' It is what some may refer to as the Bananarama effect; 'It ain't what you do it's the way that you do it'. Four of the proposed leadership styles – visionary, coaching, affiliative and democratic – create a resonance or positive emotions which boost individual and organisational performance. The styles build this resonance through focusing on shared dreams, connecting people's goals to organisational ones, connecting people to each other and valuing people through participation, respectively. Two further styles – pacesetting and commanding – had very specific uses in meeting challenging goals and calming fears by giving clear instructions in a crisis. They should be used with care, as sadly their overuse led to a largely negative impact on too many organisations; what the authors termed dissonance. This command and control style of leadership, predominantly using one of the two dissonance styles, leads to a negative climate and declining or poor performance.

I first studied the various leadership styles on the Leadership Programme for Serving Headteachers. I was struck by how subtle changes in behaviours could lead to quite significant changes in impact. Changing a statement into a question; obtaining multiple potential solutions to a problem and then examining each one for its relative merits; being clear about end points but giving much greater ownership to colleagues of the process or journey to achieving it; or creating opportunities to lead rather than giving people tasks to do, are all simple examples of how leaders may create greater resonance.

It is the ability to explicitly determine the set of leadership behaviours required at a particular time, in a particular situation and in a particular context that enables successful strategy. Understanding the six different leadership styles, how to adapt and merge them if necessary, and the automaticity with which they can be used comes with practice and experience. Central to developing as a leader is a willingness to look at your own performance; where it is strong and what needs to be developed, and then enacting improvements. The leadership styles provide a means of doing this and a platform from which decisions and actions may be made.

Repeating patterns of change

Leading change in response to either internal or external forces is a key component of a leader's work. It may be that leaders believe there is something the organisation could or should do much better or a response to external events is required. These changes 'can be understood as movement across a landscape of possibility' (Reeves et al., 2018). In *Your Change Needs a Strategy*, Reeves proposed five repeating patterns through which change may be put into practice. In reading them it is worth noting to what extent the end point and the means are pre-determined and to what extent they are determined by the leader or group. It can help leaders prepare for the journey ahead and determine which particular strategy is the best fit for a specific purpose. I would summarise them as:

		Means	
		Clearly defined	Not defined
Endpoints	Clearly defined	*Planned itinerary*	*River crossing*
	Unclear	*Hill climbing*	*Scouting and wandering*

Planned itinerary is most akin to the standard development planning, school improvement or raising achievement approach seen in many schools. There is a precisely planned path with both the endpoints and the means of getting there clearly defined. Leaders tend to be single minded in implementation. Efficiency is key and resource allocation tends to be fixed at the start of the process. This leads to one-way internal communication from the top down ensuring clarity.

River crossing has a clearly defined endpoint; to get safely to the other side. However, the means of doing this is uncertain and as yet undefined. The organisation or team cross the river by feeling for the stones. It is very much one step at a time. The leader or team needs to maintain a mindset that is fixed on the endpoint but open to experimenting with how best to get there. Piloting different small-scale approaches before determining which ones to scale up, following careful assessment of the outcomes, is an appropriate approach. Resource allocation remains flexible and follows the evidence. Many school leaders will have used this approach throughout the COVID-19 pandemic.

With *hill climbing*, the means is known but the end point is uncertain. A great example of this was schools switching to online learning when the pandemic closed schools for the majority of pupils. The internet of things (different interconnected devices and users), cloud computing with its almost unlimited storage potential, and high broadband width connectivity were the means. Exactly where this new use of technology might end up in terms of future use is difficult to determine. Hence, there is a need for upward communication about what is working and how to keep things moving uphill.

Leaders sometimes need to give permission to innovate, enabling people to try out low cost, low regret actions. With *scouting and wandering* neither the endpoints nor the means are well defined. An example of this is teacher-led disciplined enquiry and development work that leads to incremental improvement. A couple of years ago, the Trust decided to give all teachers the equivalent of five additional days of non-contact time per annum to work on something of interest to them. We referred to it as enhanced personal professional development. It was messy and some teachers were better at using the time well than others. The work varied but included classroom trials, cross-phase curriculum development, and engagement in Master's qualifications. There are a number of major organisations which give staff paid time in which to innovate, with some remarkable results.

When *escaping the swamp* there is a need for substantial and urgent change, with a move to 'anywhere but here' being an immediate goal. This leads to fast acting and dramatic change. At its most effective it is a series of changes, occurring over a short timescale, with clearly defined and centrally driven endpoints and means. It is the JFDI style of leadership. It may be considered akin to the *planned itinerary* strategy but operates as a series of short sprints rather than as the single long-term plan. Leaders need to balance courage, honesty and diplomacy. Courage to act boldly, honesty to see the situation as it is and develop a sense of urgency within the organisation, and diplomacy to communicate the urgency without creating unnecessary panic that will see staff heading for the exit.

Within an organisation it is possible that all four, possibly five, strategies are in operation at the same time. It is for leaders to determine the most appropriate strategy for a particular situation or issue and maintain processes for transitioning from one to another.

Effectively engaging governors

A key role of governance is providing strategic direction to the organisation. For many of the big moves, leaders will need the support of the governing body. Some due to the governing body's role as employers in a number of schools, and others due to the counter-cultural nature of what you might be proposing. Some things are sufficiently risky to constitute foolishness if implemented by a lone leader in the absence of oversight and challenge from governors, and when necessary, their explicit permission.

When I look back on my spreadsheets and graphs of lesson grades, they now appear as ancient history. Less than a decade ago, grading teachers' lessons was the perceived wisdom, and governors expected this kind of data. Moving away from this earlier than most schools was a leap of faith and required taking the governing body with me. They had been used to the data; they believed it and believed it was the key to school improvement. It was necessary to re-educate the governors in the same way that I had needed to re-educate myself, senior leaders and even the teachers on the receiving end of this madness. Change has to be a process over time, not an event announced at one meeting. The latter feels like a hi-jack and may elicit a negative reaction from the very people you are seeking to guide and work with.

When first appointed headteacher at St. Mary's, I instituted an additional annual joint governing body and senior leadership development planning meeting, as part of the development planning cycle. It was a great way for people to put names to faces, develop a bit of rapport and work together to develop the plan. In the early years it consisted of signing off the annual budget and discussions which were largely tactical in nature rather than truly strategic. However, within a few years they started to become genuinely strategic. At different annual development planning meetings, we considered, among other things: the OECD's six future school scenarios; whether to look at developing a MAT or participate in the combined BSF/PCP capital plan; LKMCo's *The Talent Challenge* (commissioned by Oceanova); and the part the research school would play in school improvement, locally, regionally and internally. It was part of developing the people – governors and senior leaders – as well as the organisation.

Capitalising your assets

I certainly could not describe the moment as a high point in my career. The first set of accounts was being prepared for the multi-academy trust, and I was asked whether I wanted to capitalise our assets. I can still remember thinking that I did not care much nor had I come into teaching to answer questions like that. However, as the CEO of the Trust it was a reasonable question to be asked, and it was one that needed an answer. Capitalising assets is a process used by accountants to spread the costs of an asset over a number of years rather than the full cost appearing as an outgoing in the year in which it was purchased. The asset is added to the balance sheet and depreciated over its lifetime. It has the benefit of spreading out major purchases, and in the decade past, when austerity hit education hard, it probably helped some Trusts remain solvent.

Like many Catholic schools, when we converted to a multi-academy trust the Diocese retained ownership of the land and rented it back to the school. We had no land and building assets to offset our share of the millions of pounds of deficit in the local authority's pension pot relating to support staff. This deficit had been transferred to the Trust when staff moved over into its employment, and now the Trust was technically insolvent. Understanding both these issues meant neither of them kept me awake at night. This enhanced knowledge of a range of inter-related domains, was critical in keeping myself sane and helping form the Blessed Edward Bamber Catholic Multi-Academy Trust, otherwise known as BEBCMAT.

Forming the multi-academy trust was a very long process rather than an event. In about 2005, I was invited onto a specialist schools and academies trust system redesign group with some really interesting school leaders (I always had a deep sense of imposter syndrome). One of the leaders was Dave Harris, the headteacher of Serlby Park, who invited me to visit him and his school. It was an all through school, a fairly rare beast in the state sector in those days. Walking in I was asking myself the question, 'Why would you do this?' Five hours later my question was, 'Why would you not do this?' It was the start of a decade long journey that led to the formation of BEBCMAT.

As previously mentioned, one key event occurred in 2009 when St. Mary's hard federated with Christ the King, with one governing body responsible for the two schools. It was where a sense of direction aligned with unfolding events on the ground. Big strategic moves like this link together our mission – why we exist, our values – what we believe in and how we will behave, and vision – what we want to be. In essence it is about 'walking the talk' or implementing the thought. Hamel and Prahalad, in the *Harvard Business Review* (1989), describe it as reconciling 'ends to means through strategic intent'. There are three elements of strategic intent: a sense of direction, a sense of discovery and a sense of destiny.

A sense of direction implies a particular vision of the future, which needs to be both unifying and personalised. A sense of discovery involves exploring new territory, differentiating the organisation from others, thus creating its unique selling point. And a sense of destiny brings an emotional edge to the strategy; the belief that what you are doing is inherently worthwhile. The process of forming the Trust was mission, values and vision laden, and over time, I experienced that sense of direction, discovery and destiny.

A sense of destiny

In late 2013 the governors started the process of appointing an executive headteacher for September 2014. The issue was on the agenda of a full governing body meeting. At the point the governors were going to discuss the appointment, I expressed an interest and left the meeting, advising them to advertise nationally. Later, I discovered that a number of the governors struggled with the idea of advertising the post, they felt I was doing a good job and wanted to just appoint me. These can be difficult moments for both governors and headteachers. For what it is worth, I also thought I was doing a good job, but the executive headteacher role was different to the one I had been doing for the past thirteen years. It was important that the governing body had the best person to fill the new role, not just a good one. If I was the best person for the job than I believed I would be duly appointed, if not, I accepted that I would probably be made redundant and would seek a new post elsewhere. When I went home and explained the appointment process to Cath, she was less than impressed.

As leaders we are only ever a link in a chain. We hold the stewardship of an organisation for a period of time, but the organisation existed and was led both before us, and will be after our tenure. This endeavour was much bigger than one person, and it just felt much more important than me and my career. Fortunately, after the national advert and interview I was appointed as the executive headteacher of the hard federated schools.

In deep partnership working, the issue of who leads is often the elephant in the room. Often, we feel more comfortable in shallow partnerships that allow us maximum autonomy rather than surrendering some of our authority. It is undoubtedly easier for me to hold this view given I was the person who had the position of greatest professional authority in the Trust. Discussions among school leaders looking to form a multi-academy trust are often concerned with the proposed leadership structure. Linking back to Hamel and Prahalad, a sense of direction implies a particular vision of the future which needs to be both unifying and personalised. There is a necessary trade-off of individual autonomy for shared autonomy and the greater professional capital of the group.

The final part of the Trust jigsaw came together in September 2014 when St. Cuthbert's joined St. Mary's and Christ the King in forming a multi-academy trust. Christ the King had gone from strength to strength as a school, and it was interesting to watch Sarah, the headteacher, become the key leader in helping move St. Cuthbert's forward. The work she led significantly enhanced the quality of education offered to children, and Christ the King, the school that had received so much from working in partnership, was now the school giving the most.

The formation of the cross-phase BEBCMAT was mission focused. We came together to work together, to work in communion supporting and helping strengthen each of the schools, and in particular the school that was in greatest difficulty at that moment in time. This underpins my view with respect to the governance of Catholic schools. The one governing body to one school is the least preferential model as it puts us in silos. I am not particularly an advocate of the multi-academy trust model as I feel the hard federated model worked equally as well. There are schools that do excellent work supporting other schools outside of a formal governance structure, I simply see it as a way of maximising the benefits of aligning form and function.

Mainly because we were the only Catholic multi-academy trust in the North West of England, I would receive requests to speak to leaders who were thinking of establishing a multi-academy trust. Occasionally, I also spoke at conferences and some Diocesan meetings. These are the questions I would ask people to reflect on:

- What do you want to achieve from forming or joining a multi-academy trust? What can you do better together than you can do as separate organisations?
- What can you offer to other schools within the multi-academy trust?
- What would you be willing to give up to be part of the multi-academy trust?
- What pain will you take for other schools and school leaders?

Leaders almost never had an adequate answer to the first question and had given little thought to the others. Jumping before you are pushed is not a sufficient reason to form a multi-academy trust or any other long-term deep partnership. Multi-academy trusts are not a single thing. While basically the same legal entity, multi-academy trusts differ from one another quite significantly. Determining why, as a group of schools, you want to come together, what it is you want to achieve, has to precede what your structure may be. The decision to come together is only a start; making it happen requires a group of people with tenacity and a wide range of skills.

Managing the risks

Formal risk management had not been part of my usual leadership approach. Spotting the odd iceberg as it came towards me neatly summed up my own and most school leaders' view of risk management. It was not until I had been through the Building Schools for the Future programme that the potential benefits of identifying, assessing and mitigating risks in advance was established in my mind. The risk management process is a component of the planning phase and should also be on-going throughout a project. Once you have been initiated in risk management plans, it is relatively natural to consider them more informally when leading smaller projects. Forethought is always better than emergency firefighting.

When forming the hard federation in 2009, governors briefly gave thought to forming an all through school, and an assessment of the financial impact of this was fully considered. In the school funding formula of the time, the impact on a school's budget of forming an all through school was significant. The funding formula allocated each school, regardless of its size, a lump sum of around £150,000 per annum. Instead of two lump sums, one for primary and one for the secondary, the all through school would have received one, resulting in a loss of about £150,000 every year. It challenged us to really think about what we wanted to achieve in bringing the two schools together. What we actually wanted and needed was a perspective and approach to all through education rather than the coming together of two schools into a single legal identity. Unwary schools discovered the financial loss only after coming together, so the risk management process was essential, not simply a nice to have.

A risk management process involves identification of risks, an assessment of the potential quantum of a risk and examining ways of mitigating it. Throughout the formation of the multi-academy trust, I maintained and shared a risk assessment register with the shadow trust board, which had been formed to ensure governor oversight of the process. The risk register consisted of the following sections: governance, standards, finance, premises, staffing and human resources. The latter section looked at legal risks associated with moving employees over to the multi-academy trust. The legal firm guiding us through the academisation process provided us with a number of key issues for the risk register. Others were added at meetings as new or previously unseen risks were identified. Each risk was assessed on the basis of two different factors: likelihood and impact. A scale of one to four was used for each factor. One was assigned to risks that were either unlikely to happen or would have limited impact, scaling up to four for risks that were certain or highly likely or would have a significant impact on the formation or performance of the Trust. The two assigned scores were then multiplied together, giving a range of potential overall risks from 1 (very low) to 16 (very high).

There is an element of judgement required in deciding how much time and resource to allocate to mitigation of each risk. A direct hit from a meteor strike on the schools would have been devastating (massive impact) but the likelihood is so low no time or effort was given to it. However, a negative Ofsted inspection, while potentially only slightly less devastating, is highly likely in areas of significant socio-economic disadvantage like Blackpool. Mitigation was needed.

Concerns about standards were in part mitigated by overstaffing the schools in advance of forming the multi-academy trust. We also appointed a few key staff to lead the development of a whole Trust curriculum from 5 to 16 years old in core subjects, extending this to other subjects over time. It proved to be strategically fortuitous given the change in direction of the latest inspection framework. With respect to governance, we identified concerns relating to a lack of clear direction during the academisation process or once the multi-academy trust was formed, and around failure to make timely decisions. This was mitigated by establishing the shadow trust board twelve months in advance of academisation. We sent out regular updates on progress and decisions concerning academisation to all staff.

The risk register was maintained and updated on a spreadsheet. This allowed for changes to the scores assigned to each identified risk to be easily updated as matters were resolved or mitigated or increased. The overall score for each risk was also shown in graphical form, which always drew your eye to the big risks. Two issues that had red flashing lights associated with them related to equal pay and the children's centre.

Equal Pay had been triggered following a national campaign and a series of court victories by female employees against local authorities (the employers). It was a decades old gender based issue associated with support staff serving in different roles: learning support assistants compared to site supervisors compared to administrative and technical staff. Roles traditionally undertaken by men were afforded higher rates of pay. Further, a number of jobs traditionally done by men received an odd additional payment called plusage (a salary uplift) which served to increase the low wage to a higher value, whereas women were just expected to accept the lower wage.

Key to understanding the issue was identifying who the 'single source' employer was. This is the employer who ultimately employees the people and who can right the wrong. For a voluntary-aided school, the governing body is the single source employer. For a community or voluntary controlled school, it is the local authority. Comparisons could be made within the whole organisation across all the different roles employees did, but not between employees in different organisations. By 2013/14 equal pay was on many school leaders' agendas. For community and voluntary controlled schools the matter was made more complex as comparisons could be made to other employees of the local authority, such as grave diggers, refuse workers, or residential staff. Work of equal value needed to be afforded equal pay.

As we sought to establish the multi-academy trust, there was a need to ensure equal pay for staff employed by St. Cuthbert's governing body and the hard federated governing body of St, Mary's and Christ the King. This was because BEBCMAT, who would employ all the staff from both schools, would be the new single source employer. We asked Blackpool's human resources team to use the equal pay scheme already agreed with the unions, which objectively aligned and scored different roles and responsibilities, to manage the process. This ensured that jobs of equal value would receive equal pay. Not only is this just and right but it removed the potential for litigation against the Trust. As the process was completed the risk went from flashing red lights, to amber and finally green. Further, the process taught me an invaluable leadership lesson about the emotional side of leadership, which I will return to later in the book.

The children's centre presented a different risk to the new Trust. Located on the St. Cuthbert's school site, it had been established around the start of the century. It did invaluable outreach work to support families and children, from birth and before, in an area of massive socio-economic disadvantage. It co-ordinated different educational, health and social services in one place and supported families' access to them. With austerity beginning to bite hard, the service was needed more than ever.

The children's centre was funded by a central government grant that came via the local authority, but the contract relating to the funding and expectation of the services to be provided was only for one year. The council thought it would continue but could not give concrete assurances about the continuation of funding. Staff were in post on permanent contracts, so the major risk to the Trust was that if the funding stopped it would be liable for all redundancy costs. There appeared little mitigation we could put in place, unless the shadow trust board had refused to take over the children's centre contract, which would have led to the centre's closure. In essence, we decided to carry the risk on the basis it was known and could be quantified. I had requested and received the potential redundancy costs and shared these with the shadow trust board. Sadly, one of the last things I did as CEO of BEBCMAT was to manage the closure of the children's centre. The writing was on the wall by late 2018 as the central government grant was reduced then removed.

In *Capitalising Your Assets*, I have tried to show how enhanced knowledge across a range of specialised areas – finance, human resources, risk management, legal, governance – is required by leaders. Suffice to say, I possessed little of it when I first became a headteacher. Knowledge grew with experience, and experience grew my knowledge. The Basic of Strategy is essential for school leaders if they are to bring coherence and direction to the organisation's big strategic moves.

Ways of Doing

Basic 5: Implementation

The importance of effective implementation

An effective leader ensures improvements to the organisation's ways of working and outcomes. They are adept at addressing and remedying organisational challenges and problems. This involves forming the improvement nodes associated with an organisation's structures, systems, processes and practices.

Summary

- Improvements can too often be driven by personal preference or political ideology leading to busyness and limited progress. This approach is needlessly exhausting for teachers and school leaders.
- Three key leadership dimensions need to be considered when implementing change: authority, capacity and accountability.
- Authority is concerned with the mandate given to the person leading the particular initiative. Accountability provides clarity about who is actually leading and ultimately responsible for the particular initiative, objective or process. Capacity looks at the resources required.
- Too often leaders plunge head long into significant and substantial change without sufficient thought being given to the change process, beyond the initial steps. The implementation process needs to be slowed down. This will allow the whole process to be thought about more and implemented more effectively.
- While there is a significant aspect of professional development that can be foreseen, there is also a need to build in time for aspects of professional development that emerge during the implementation of a particular initiative.
- Teachers mediate any instructional programme aimed at pupils. A teacher's beliefs based on evidence (a rationale element), feelings based on what works for them or what they prefer (a more emotional dimension), and what they have previously done (habits), will impact significantly on their motivation.
- The closer any new approach is to a teacher's beliefs, experiences and classroom habits, the greater the chance of effective implementation.
- Improvement efforts need to be part of a systematic approach. Organisations that appear to be best at getting better are judicious in choosing what to do and how to do it.
- Leaders must spend time thinking about how deep-rooted issues might be addressed. Identifying the upstream issues involves finding out why people were falling into the river in the first place, rather than pulling them out downstream (Heath, 2020).

Implementation

The standard school improvement process – certainly Blackpool's default modus operandi for many years – involved finding numerous kitchen sinks to throw at perceived problems. Randomly throw kitchen sinks with as much energy and passion as possible, have little or no impact, fall down exhausted. Repeat *ad nauseam*.

Apart from the wasted time and effort, if things did improve you simply had no idea what worked and should be continued or what did not. This approach may lead to extreme versions of the IKEA effect, where people who led the implementation or came up with the idea obviously believed in it, and sometime later they conclude it is indeed brilliant despite a lack of empirical evidence or in spite of evidence that suggests otherwise. From the classroom via the headteacher's office to the Department for Education, improvements can too often be driven by personal preference or political ideology. Our current approach leads to busyness and limited progress, and is needlessly exhausting for teachers and school leaders.

Over the time I led schools, my way of operating changed significantly, and I became increasingly ruthless in prioritising what we did. I also gave far more thought to how we were going to do it and the capacity required. Too often leaders plunge head long into significant and substantial change without sufficient thought being given to the change process, beyond the initial steps. As such, many unnecessary changes are implemented, and potentially beneficial changes are doomed to failure before they actually begin. Bergman (2018) concludes that an 'organisation's biggest strategic challenge isn't strategic thinking – it's strategic acting'. It is how to ensure 'consistent, collaborative, co-ordinated movement towards a common objective'. Schools and school leaders have become change junkies. The implementation process needs to be slowed down, which will allow the whole procedure to be thought about more and implemented more effectively.

Three key leadership dimensions need to be considered when implementing change: authority, capacity and accountability. Authority is concerned with the mandate given to the person leading the particular initiative. Accountability provides clarity about who is actually leading and ultimately responsible for the particular initiative, objective or process, they are the ultimate decision maker. For this reason I always preferred one named leader, as this helps ensure decisions are made in a timely manner. Accountability also includes how a leader will be held accountable and for what. Capacity looks at the resources required. Often when an initiative falls apart or never really gets off the ground, it is because one or more of these elements were not considered at the outset.

A fundamental aspect of capacity is time; a finite resource that may only be used once. Too many initiatives are started without a proper audit of the time needed for successful implementation, at all levels within the organisation. Professor Becky Allen once tweeted that school leaders should cost the time required for implementing a project or initiative as if the organisation would have to pay all the staff working to implement it overtime. The costs are usually very substantial. It allows a cost-benefit analysis, common in private industry and commerce, to be undertaken. Will we be getting the right bang for our bucks? Expressed differently, is this the best use of our staff's limited and finite time?

As well as the time needed, a careful assessment of the new or different capabilities (knowledge and skills) required by staff to effectively implement a new way of working is required. With the current focus on curriculum, leaders need to understand that there can be no substantial curriculum development without substantive professional development. You can replace the word 'curriculum' with any other major area that a school or organisation is intending to transform. While there is a significant aspect of professional development that can be foreseen, there is also a need to build in time for aspects of professional development that emerge during the implementation of a particular initiative. As part of this, a decision will need to be made as to whether there is a requirement to bring in external expertise. Finally, a financial – as well as time and professional development – assessment should be made.

Does the school or organisation have the capacity to implement now or do we need to delay to a future point? Is the new initiative of sufficient importance for other, now less important things, to be abandoned? As a profession we are too ready to keep adding to our work and workload rather than stopping, thinking and really prioritising. Is this a nine or a ten out of ten? If not, then it is a no. The need to do fewer things but do them much better and to greater depth is a mindset waiting to be discovered in too many schools.

Rethinking how we work

We are in a system where the speed of reaction, the 'busyness delusion', often trumps real progress. Too often leaders act with the best of intentions and the worst of thought. I can look back on a career of maximum effort, huge expenditure of energy, long hours and too little progress. Part of doing fewer things better involves slowing down the early analytical enquiry and planning phase. The foundations for better implementation require a methodical approach to improvement, and this applies equally to developing practice at a system, school and classroom level. After a conversation with Professor Stuart Kime, I blogged the following proposal as one such methodical approach:

- What's the problem?
    - Where's your evidence and how sure are you?
- What is your theory of action?
    - 'If I do x then y will happen?' Do you believe it?
- What evidence do you have to inform and challenge your logic model?
- What would it look like if you are successful?
- What information do you need to collect?
    - Baseline, during and post intervention
- Will your data help show a causal or correlation relationship?

Frustratingly, leaders too often set out to solve problems that do not exist or are peripheral to the central issue that needs addressing, so problem identification needs rigorous analysis and thought. During a coaching session, I remember being appropriately challenged to justify the rationale for identifying the particular issue we were discussing. The coach provided counter evidence that required me to think more deeply about the issue. That challenge moved me from making generalisations to a more nuanced and precise analysis of what needed to be addressed.

The next stage in the process involves developing a theory of action, which is relatively easy and quite revealing. For example, if you want to improve standards in the organisation you might propose, 'If all middle/senior leaders completed NPQML/NPQSL (National Professional Qualification for Middle Leaders/Senior Leaders) then standards, in terms of pupils' attainment and progress, will improve'. This needs to pass your common-sense test. Do you actually think this is true? There is the need to look for evidence of the efficacy of the qualifications to support the proposed theory of change. Are there other alternatives, either different training approaches or alternative actions which might improve standards? This might feel a rather slow and laborious process, but schools will improve faster if we stop doing many things that have little impact, in favour of doing fewer things that have more. From an ethical perspective, leaders should question whether a particular approach is likely to work before imposing it on all pupils in a school or across the system. Leaders need to sort the school improvement wheat from the chaff.

Once you have decided what might be the best improvement strategy, think about what success would look like and decide on how you will evidence this. Too often leaders are guilty of not even attempting to check whether what they are doing is having an impact. It does not have to be complex; the smaller the scale, the simpler the evaluation design should be. However, too many projects lack any basic kind of evaluation. The evaluation process should always be determined at the outset. Leaders' attempts to try to retrofit an evaluation design are invariably undone by a lack of baseline data. In addition to assessments produced or collated by teachers, there are a variety of national reference tests and standardised attitudinal surveys that can be used for evaluative purposes. It takes a bit of time and thought, but this is a disciplined enquiry style approach that professionals should engage in. Showing a causal relationship will require larger randomised control tests and professional support, but looking at any correlation between action and effect would be a huge step forward.

The Bananarama principle …

It's the way that you do it, that's what gets results.

There is a fascinating and apparently well-known study in research circles called *Project Follow Through*. It started in the 1960s and showed the problem of replication in education. For an approach to be considered reliable we would need to see broadly similar results repeated over time and in different contexts. The 'what you do' makes a difference. The project looked at the impact on children's achievement of over a dozen philosophically different instructional models of early childhood education. The problem for the evaluation team was that their findings showed a greater difference in achievement within each programme than between the different programmes (House *et al.*, 1978). Direct instruction, co-operative learning and phonics, in the wrong hands, are all pretty ineffective, whereas in the right hands they can have real impact. It may not be as simple as ensuring sufficient or improved training in how to implement. A teacher's belief in an approach's efficacy may affect implementation as much as their technical skills; for better or worse. Add to the mix the complexity of thirty little human beings in a classroom, and system wide school improvement becomes even more complex.

When implementing anything, and more so when scaling up beyond the initial trial or attempt, there needs to be fidelity to the approach being used. Without it we invalidate the attempt to link the intervention and the effect. Fidelity requires an instructional approach to be implemented within limits, and although these limits require the core of the approach to be respected, they do permit some allowable variation by a teacher. Teachers mediate any instructional programme aimed at pupils. A teacher's beliefs based on evidence (a rationale element), feelings based on what works for them or what they prefer (a more emotional dimension), and what they have previously done (habits), will impact significantly on their motivation. The closer any new approach is to a teacher's beliefs, experiences and classroom habits, the greater the chance of effective implementation.

Given the part a teacher plays in the success or failure of a particular approach, allowing them greater agency in choosing areas of their own practice to improve or new pedagogical approaches to implement, from a range of best or better alternative bets, may have significant advantages. It is a whole different way of thinking and working; busyness out and real progress in.

I am tending towards the view that although we do have enough time for high quality school improvement, we are just not using it very well. Slow, steady, thoughtful and sustainable improvement is possible if we are focused on a few high leverage interventions effectively implemented.

Getting better at getting better

Improvement efforts need to be part of a systematic approach. Organisations that appear to be best at getting better are judicious in choosing what to do and how to do it; they are inquisitive about findings but not precious about ideas, unless they show evidence of working. They avoid attribution errors and do not confuse correlation with causation. They commit to the long-term view of improvement unless they are escaping the swamp or where interim evidence suggests limited impact and little potential for improvement. Fidelity is a key factor during implementation and is the focus of training, monitoring, observing, feedback and coaching. These organisations tend to be outward facing. They show an informed interest in the wider body of research evidence available but understand its limitations. Laboratory based research deliberately tries to isolate and control variables, it seeks to simplify the context to enable causal relationships to be formed. The classroom environment is inherently complex, which means careful thought must be given to the application of research in schools and its scaling up at a system level.

It may be wise for organisations and their leaders to choose to work with research evidence that is well established, where the evidence has stood the test of time and been implemented in various contexts. Having a few members of staff who have a more detailed, nuanced understanding of the limitations of research in general and specific pieces in detail is important. Research into a particular issue can at times be contradictory. Creating a meta-analysis is one way to overcome the difficulties but leads to other problems, as research collated into a meta-analysis combines separate, often disparate pieces of research into a single conclusion with the consequence that important subtleties may be lost. This is probably why experts in their field are content to embrace a level of uncertainty when formulating conclusions and recommendations; they do not always require the certainty that comes with implementing something in a certain way. I appreciate experts who bring a common-sense approach to suggestions about the what and the how of implementation, they are well worth listening too.

Putting evidence to work

The Education Endowment Foundation (EEF) is a charity that has been part of a significant movement and improvement in a more evidence-informed approach to school improvement. Many school leaders and teachers will be familiar with their *Teaching and Learning Toolkit*. The toolkit consists of a series of teaching approaches that have been evaluated on the basis of the cost of implementation, the strength of the evidence supporting the approach, and the estimated impact in terms of additional months of progress gained.

In addition, the EEF produces a series of guidance reports to support the teaching of literacy, mathematics, science and learning behaviours, including one entitled *Putting Evidence to Work – A School's Guide to Implementation* (EEF, 2019). Two specific recommendations within the report relate to the culture and climate of the improvement process. Namely, 'Treat implementation as a process, not an event; plan and execute it in stages' and 'Create a leadership environment and school climate that is conducive to good implementation'.

The guidance paper proposed a four-stage process; Explore, Prepare, Deliver, Sustain:

- Explore – Define the problem you want to solve and identify appropriate programmes or practices to implement.
- Prepare – Create a clear implementation plan, judge the readiness of the school to deliver that plan, then prepare staff and resources.
- Deliver – Support staff, monitor progress, solve problems, and adapt strategies as the approach is used for the first time.
- Sustain – Plan for sustaining and scaling an intervention from the outset and continuously acknowledge and nurture its use.

The process starts by identifying what the problem is. Obtaining data, both quantitative and qualitative to identify the real issue is key. This was brought home to me most acutely when I sat in a Blackpool Opportunity Area meeting in September 2017. The meeting was analysing another disappointing set of GCSE results where English was particularly poor and more so for white disadvantaged boys. In reality, white disadvantaged boys' performance in GCSE English is poor across the country, but Blackpool just has a disproportionately higher number hence their greater impact on overall results.

The gender and disadvantage gap in GCSE English has remained alarmingly stable over the years, with girls outperforming boys by 0.84, 0.82 and 0.79 of a grade respectively from 2017 to 2019. More affluent pupils outperformed their disadvantaged peers (FSM Ever6) by 1.10, 1.14 and 1.10 of a grade over the same time period. There has been no national outcry about these results, even though they represent the most significant attainment gender gap in the system. We may occasionally talk about it, but we are not systematically acting on it. These GCSE English results were a downstream problem, and quick wins were deemed essential. Blackpool schools made a bee line for their English departments, but the underlying issue was and still is literacy levels across the curriculum.

Exploring underlying systemic problems

The heroic Year 6 and Year 11 teachers often pull it out of the bag. Against seemingly impossible odds they manage to achieve results that are either a huge relief or a genuine source of pride. The long hours, high workload, extra stress and additional or targeted interventions are a downstream way of life; saving pupils, particularly the most disadvantaged, from drowning in poor results.

The start of year discussions with middle leaders, the examination season post-mortem, is a standard part of a school's year. The format and tone can vary significantly between organisations, and I had been approaching them for many years as a 'find out and fix' diagnostic style process. The September 2017 process was immediately following the implementation of the first set of revised GCSEs in English and mathematics, with many heads of departments part way through teaching the first year of the new, more heavily content laden GCSEs. Similar conversations had occurred the previous year when the now infamous Dodo question had appeared in the Key Stage 2 reading SATs. Three key issues appeared to be at the heart of the discussions:

- Poor attainment and progress at GCSE across a range of literacy-based subjects including English; white disadvantaged boys were a particular concern.
- Limited commitment or hours spent preparing for or revising for examinations.
- A lack of resilience in academic work; with increasingly challenging and complex content to master, pupils give up too easily when learning becomes hard work.

The new three Rs– Reading, Revision (Retrieval) and Resilience – became part of a co-ordinated cross-Trust school improvement effort. The issues were already in the Trust's business plan but now became much more sharply focused.

Faced with too many of these moments during my time as a leader, September 2017 was a watershed point. The role of CEO gave me the time and space to think about the deep-rooted issues and how we might address them. What Heath (2020) would describe as the upstream proactive solution of finding out why people were falling into the river in the first place, rather than pulling them out downstream. The lack of focus on getting literacy right for all pupils shows the classic upstream barriers: problem blindness, lack of ownership, and tunnelling (Heath, 2020).

For many teachers, their experience of a number of pupils struggling with literacy is a systemic issue in the classes taught, where the poor readers and writers were disproportionately boys from lower socio-economic groups. We have simply become blind to the problem of literacy and have focused on ameliorating the symptoms; edging better examination performance wherever possible.

The second barrier identified by Heath (2020) is a lack of ownership. At various points as a classroom teacher and middle leader, I can remember thinking, 'What the hell are these English teachers doing?' Literacy was the domain of the English department. I was there to teach science!

At the start of my career, literacy across the curriculum was the order of the day. The concept was right but the implementation shocking. Too often a bright young member of the English department was given their first TLR point (teaching and leadership responsibility point/management payment) with the mandate to improve literacy. These junior recruits lacked the authority, leadership knowledge and experience to make any impact. It allowed people to continue believing, 'that's not mine to fix'.

I had not seen the obvious issue of tier three (disciplinary language). I lacked the knowledge and understanding required to teach literacy. There might have been a session in my teacher training about it, I honestly cannot remember, but it did not form a significant aspect of any professional development. In our Trust, pre-teaching vocabulary was pretty standard across all our primary staff, it was considered a major pedagogical advance when suggested to secondary teachers, English and modern foreign language teachers aside.

Heath's (2020) final barrier is one of tunnelling. The greatest scarcity many people have in their work is time, and with limited time, focusing on the immediate aspect of the job becomes the overriding priority; 'In the tunnel there is only forward'. This will be familiar to many people working in schools, where tunnelling leads to us focusing on short-term reactive thinking. Smaller issues crowd out the bigger ones; 'I must teach this in my lesson today or we will not be ready for next week's test'. This can lead to major problems associated with a lack of literacy or a lack of significant prior knowledge, being left unaddressed.

There is a point at which addressing the few really important issues has to take priority over the urgent. If not, we will spend our careers trying to stop people drowning downstream by pulling them out of the river.

It's literacy, stupid

Improving pupils' literacy is a no-brainer. Ensuring children and young people are functionally literate and able to access the curriculum are good things and something all schools, teachers and parents can sign up to. The problem is that not all children and young people are, and those from disadvantaged backgrounds are far more likely to struggle with literacy than their more advantaged peers. Blackpool is an area of extreme long-term disadvantage, containing eight of the ten most deprived areas in the whole of England and Wales. Many children start school well behind their age expected development. Poor speech, communication and language skills, limited vocabulary and life experiences all make reading more difficult, particularly comprehension and inference. This has a knock-on effect to accessing the curriculum.

Exploring the problem

It is difficult to know where to start when faced with a problem as overwhelming as poor literacy. Some things we did know, for example analysis of Key Stage 2 reading data showed that comprehension (inference) was a particular weakness for our pupils on entering secondary school. However, knowing one aspect of the problem does not mean you have identified them all, nor does it mean you have a grasp of the most important issues or the sequence in which the issues need to be addressed.

Teaching reading initially links letters to word sounds. There is then a need to develop word meaning, expand vocabulary and ensure correct spelling. Children need to gain reading fluency and comprehend what they are reading. The latter requires knowledge of syntactic rules to help interpret particular sentences, and this in turn links to understanding ideas across sentences. It is a complex and highly specialised area. There are probably only a few teachers in each school who possess this detailed knowledge, and they are often found in Early Years and Key Stage 1. Every teacher needs a working knowledge of how children learn to read and then get better at reading. Substantial professional development is required to ensure all teachers can help pupils gain the master skill of reading, as it is a prerequisite to accessing the curriculum. My knowledge of the whole process was very, very limited.

Fortunately, for the cost of a lunch, Professor Philippa Cordingley started to fill in some significant gaps in my knowledge and understanding of reading. Simon Eccles, the headteacher at St. Mary's, was already fully engaged in developing the school-wide literacy project with me. Graeme Duncan and Paul O'Neill from Right to Succeed, a charity we had built up a relationship with over a number of years, started linking us up with organisations who would be able to support the project. Later on, Lexonik and GL Assessment would be central to the project's forward momentum. We were beginning to unite the right people; wrapping a team around the problem. Unwittingly but with perfect timing, Professor Daniel T. Willingham published *The Reading Mind: A Cognitive Approach to How the Mind Reads* in 2017.

Preparing the ground

Too often when major initiatives or projects are started, they come as a total surprise to the staff. Announced on an Inset day or written into a development plan, teachers are expected to change an aspect of classroom practice with little forewarning and often less professional development or coaching support. By this stage of my career, I had tried this 'out of the blue' approach and too often failed to have the impact I'd hoped for. I set myself the timescale of six months for thinking and planning how we would improve pupils' ability to read. The six-month period was September 2017 to February 2018. Simon always counselled that such a fundamental change would need the full academic year. He was right, six months was at best overly optimistic. At worst it would have left us significantly under prepared for what turned out to be a massive undertaking. High quality implementation always seems to take longer than I initially think it will.

The process started gently. I basically presented back to staff from across the Trust the three Rs – Reading, Revision (Retrieval) and Resilience – telling them that if these were the root causes, we were going to 'go big' on trying to address them. I implored them to speak up if we had identified the wrong issues. No-one did. As a leader you can never be sure whether this is because the correct issues have been identified, people are too busy to respond or simply exhausted by yet another school improvement idea. Either way we continued.

The next stage was pulling together a short-term cross-Trust working party to start the process of exploring ideas and what might form key strands of our approach. We used the EEF's *Teaching and Learning Toolkit* as a starting point, identifying reading comprehension strategies as useful; a moderate impact intervention for very low cost with extensive evidence behind them. We later understood that reading comprehension skills tend to give a one-off but significant boost. Once pupils are taught how to use them, to continue to teach them does not appear to lead to much more improvement.

A member of staff visited various schools to look at their use of Accelerated Reader, a reading programme that aims to foster the habit of independent reading among primary and early secondary age pupils. We decided it was not for us and chose a literary canon approach. Later in the project, Accelerated Reader was adopted by a number of Blackpool schools when the project went town-wide. One size does not fit all, but the key principle was to ensure all pupils spent more time reading.

It helps massively if people understand the rationale behind why something is being done. Engaging them in the early thinking and exploring some ideas also helps lower stress levels when more fully formed plans start to be rolled out. Reducing the scale of the change can help with this. Utilising this approach, another group met to look specifically at the pre-teaching of vocabulary in secondary classrooms. As part of the process, we visited both a history and a science lesson. In one I asked a pupil what she had thought of the teacher's approach of pre-teaching the key vocabulary used in the lesson. Her response was revealing, 'I really liked it. I know what's going on now, it is not like my other lessons'; out of the mouths of babes. I wonder how many pupils sit in lessons listening to teachers speaking in highly specialised language with little grasp of what is actually being said.

Alongside my, by now standard, 'Are these three Rs the big issues we should be focusing on?' I offered to purchase a copy of *The Reading Mind* (Willingham, 2017) for any member of staff who wanted to read it. There would be the option of coming together after school, on a couple of occasions, to discuss what we had read. This approach is a really cheap but effective form of professional development, and the simple process of reading Willingham's book was significant.

Many teachers were honest about their lack of ownership of literacy; rooted in limited knowledge and understanding of how to teach it. Through reading the book, they started understanding some important aspects of it: the importance of decoding and the part phonics played in reading; the need for greater fluency and an extended vocabulary; the requirement for more time to be spent reading in school, dedicated reading time and opportunities in lessons were both important; and the need for sufficient background knowledge to understand the text fully. One of the things that many staff said was either 'I wish I had known this when my children were growing up' or 'This is really useful and will help me with my child'. Interest had been piqued, and the chance of all teachers supporting literacy had been significantly increased. The ground had been prepared for some of the more difficult challenges ahead, and many more staff now had an appreciation of how they contributed to the overall literacy picture within the school and the Trust.

The elements of the literacy programme were now beginning to take shape:

- Fluent decoding: phonics instruction, spelling instruction and reading practice.
- Comprehension: depth and breadth of vocabulary (Tier two and three words); reading comprehension strategies and prior background knowledge that required systematic and sequential curriculum planning.
- A slightly more ephemeral set of thoughts around motivation. Reading as an emotional choice, rooted in our past experiences, expectancy value theory and reading self-concept (Willingham, 2017).

The Key Stage 3 literacy (reading) project

From March 2018, the literacy project was scaled up at the request of the Blackpool Opportunity Area. All secondary schools and the Pupil Referral Units were invited to take part, and there followed a couple of meetings and a series of emails to get feedback on the draft plan. By this stage, I had gained considerable knowledge, and with the support of others I wrote a sufficiently detailed framework for the project. Very few amendments were suggested. What school and Trust leaders wanted most was clarity around what was expected of them.

The CEOs of all the Blackpool secondary schools and the headteacher of the PRU signed letters of commitment to their involvement in the project. This idea of formally contracting with people is important, as organisations need clarity about the income, support and expectations of any programme they engage in, if they are to make informed decisions about their capacity to successfully engage. The same is true when considering competing priorities within an organisation. The initial cost of the two-year Key Stage 3 Literacy programme was just under £1 million. It was paid for by Opportunity Area funds and philanthropy raised by Right to Succeed. The project was extended for a further two years with the total funding being closer to £1.8 million over the four years. The project funding was primarily focused on having knowledgeable, disciplined and enthusiastic leadership in each of the schools. This was critical if it was to succeed.

The project was deliberately costed to ensure that there was sufficient funding to build capacity in schools. Far too often school improvement projects fund external organisations or consultants but expect schools to deliver with no extra funding. Failing to adequately identify the additional capacity required for any improvement undermines efforts from the outset. Half of the funding was targeted at the appointment of a senior leader (Assistant Headteacher L10-14 including on-costs) for two days a week, for the duration of the project.

The right people with the right amount of time

There were two elements to the senior leadership role, and both had associated job descriptions. One role was focused on leading and managing literacy in Key Stage 3, though we knew from the outset a number of the interventions would naturally be taken into Key Stage 4. The other role involved leading a culture shift around school improvement efforts. The role was titled the Evidence Informed Lead. The key aspect of this role was to increase capacity by reducing the number of improvement initiatives the school was engaged in. This was to be achieved through using evidence to question what the school was currently doing. The intention was to free up capacity to do fewer things but do them better, which is the opposite approach to throwing everything including the kitchen sink at school improvement. The senior leaders needed to be able to influence whole school decision making, and the literacy project was a vehicle for long-term cultural change in how we approached school improvement in Blackpool.

Schools took different approaches to the appointment: one person for the two days with the roles combined; two people for one day a week with the roles kept separate; redesigning a current senior leader's role or appointing an additional person to the senior leadership team. The key was that all the school leads had the authority and capacity to implement the project effectively. A useful side point was that the project could also insist on all senior leaders attending the required meetings and training. In essence, they had been seconded to the project two days a week.

The two days a week equated to about seventy-eight days a year. About seventeen days were used in the first year for training and meetings with fewer in the following year. There were regular in-school fortnightly or monthly meetings with a project manager from Right to Succeed, who managed the project on a day-to-day basis. Over half the time was used to implement the project at a school level. Looking back, I can see that over the years, I simply tried to implement too many projects, at the same time, without an accurate assessment of the capacity – the time and capabilities – that had to be developed.

Following the Opportunity Area and Right to Succeed boards agreeing to the project and the funding, we approached Alex Quigley to become the project's critical friend and David Weston of the Teacher Development Trust to provide training for the senior leads in what high quality professional development looked like.

Rather than a single problem associated with reading, we identified several different issues that would need to be addressed. The problems associated with pupils included the previously mentioned poor attainment and progress at GCSE across a range of literacy-based subjects including English, particularly for white disadvantaged boys. Analysis of Key Stage 2 reading data showed comprehension (inference) was a particular weakness. For a number of pupils, poor sentence and paragraph comprehension due to poor decoding skills, limited fluency and limited vocabulary were also a concern. There was also a very variable culture of reading among pupils. It was important to think beyond the issues identified for pupils and give thought to potential barriers to implementing the project that related to teachers. Limited ownership of literacy by teachers across the curriculum had led to a lack of consistency or whole school practice in the teaching of reading. This was in a large part due to teachers' limited knowledge and understanding of the teaching of reading, and more generally, literacy.

It felt overwhelming to consider them all at once, so we developed a multi-year, carefully sequenced and well-resourced plan. It took into account the day-to-day priorities of planning, teaching and assessment alongside the other long-term priorities schools had. The plan was written up in the form of a logic model.

A logic model consists of a series of columns and sub-headings that take you through the process required to effectively explore, prepare, deliver and sustain a major school improvement project (EEF, 2019). Below the contents of the Key Stage 3 literacy (reading) project are provided, with its key headings: problem; intervention description (what are the active ingredients?); intervention activities; intervention outcomes (note the sub-heading – fidelity) and pupil outcomes. Some of the sections below are from the original plan I authored:

Intervention description (What are the active ingredients?)
Active ingredient 1 – Decoding and fluency.
- Implement a phonics-based programme to improve decoding and fluency (includes aspects of orthography, morphology, etymology and semantics).

Active ingredient 2 – Vocabulary.
- Consistently implement bespoke and whole school interventions aimed at extending students' Tier two and three vocabulary.

Active ingredient 3 – Reading practice.
- Implement a programme of frequent reading for students, as part of a whole school approach.

Active ingredient 4 – Whole staff training.
- Specific staff to receive bespoke training on chosen interventions.
- Named senior leaders to receive focused training on literacy, evidence-based practice, implementation processes and CPD.
- All staff to receive training on decoding, approaches to teach vocabulary and approaches to reading.

Active ingredient 5 – Consistent approach to reading a text.
• School led process to develop a high quality consistent approach to reading a text across curriculum subjects.

Active ingredient 6 – Building capacity
• Development and implementation of systems and processes across each school based on a more evidence-informed approach.

Choosing the active ingredients of a project has a significant impact on its likely future success. It requires a mental shift from a focus on the complex problem of literacy (reading) to identifying the complicated constituent parts which may be acted on (Allen, 2019). For this project, decoding and fluency; vocabulary; increased time spent reading and a consistent approach to reading a text were the constituent parts. The latter two on the list led to substantial work on disciplinary literacy from the second year of the project onwards. Over the life of the project there was a gradual move from implementing literacy interventions to literacy being a central component of the teaching culture within the school.

Implementation activities

Key to the implementation activities was a significant amount of upfront training, particularly for the senior leads from the various schools. This included: the Education Endowment Foundation's Implementation and Literacy programmes delivered by the Research School; the Centre for the Use of Research and Evidence in Education's (CUREE) Response to Intervention; and the Teacher Development Trust's associate training. In addition, there was specific training for the staff involved in delivering some of the decoding and vocabulary enhancement interventions. There was also whole staff training on aspects of reading which quickly moved from the more general insights to specific disciplinary literacy approaches. Alongside the training was an expectation that the senior leaders would act as coaches to key staff involved in implementing elements of the reading programme throughout the lifespan of the project.

On-going monitoring and evaluation was provided by the senior leads and externally by Right to Succeed, through a series of school-based meetings and annual evaluation reports. The senior leads monitored submission of baseline and on-going data sets and qualitative evidence. This has now led to a really useful longitudinal data set for pupils in Key Stage 3, from across Blackpool schools. In addition, CUREE provided an external review using a closed case analysis tool which gave useful qualitative insights into a number of key processes and systems operating in each of the schools, which helped target areas for further development. At a whole project level, Simon Cox (Research School at St. Mary's) led the process of evaluation.

Implementation outcomes

Unlike many projects I had led or been involved with there was a very specific focus on fidelity when implementing a number of the active ingredients. This involved a clear methodology to be written for a particular intervention, training to implement the intervention using the methodology, coaching for staff when implementing, and a series of fidelity visits. The fidelity approach is to critique how a particular intervention is being implemented rather than a criticism of the person or people implementing it. One of the identified fidelity elements was a reduction in the number of initiatives being implemented by a school. Also, where a school was implementing a new initiative or objective, the implementation processes would be based on the EEF *Implementation Guidance* (2019) that the schools' leads had received training in. The final part of the logic model contained a section on pupil outcomes.

Pupil outcomes

During the lifespan of the project we hoped to see improved reading ages, and increased sentence and paragraph comprehension scores for students engaged in the programme. We were also interested in whether improved literacy may also lead to improved social and emotional development, particularly confidence and self-efficacy. Beyond the timescale of the project, the longer-term impact was about improved access to the curriculum and examination papers leading to enhanced progress across the curriculum and improved Progress 8 scores.

The Blackpool literacy project

'Every child reading at or above their chronological age' was the tagline target we set ourselves at the very beginning of the Key Stage 3 literacy (reading) project. It is what Sinek (2009) would describe as a 'what'. Why we were doing it was not simply to improve pupils' reading ages or GCSE outcomes – though those are good things – we wanted to enhance pupils' life chances, support young people out of poverty, enable them to live longer, happier and more productive lives, and break the cycle of intergenerational poor literacy. The 'whys' have a motivating and engaging moral purpose that drives them; they pull you into the work.

From very early on we identified some key enablers and learning from the project, which may be of use when considering the implementation of whole school development. Appointing an overall project lead, ideally in place nine to twelve months prior to the project's implementation start date, helped ensure the necessary decisions to get the project up and running were made in a timely manner. The actual lead in time for the project across Blackpool was only four months but significant preparatory work had been done at St. Mary's during the previous eight months, which could be transferred to the project. In leading the project, I was massively aided by a small project team of committed people who helped identify the key problems that need to be addressed, and suitable and credible active ingredients. These formed the main part of the interventions and implementation plan. Funding to support the implementation plan built significant capacity within the schools to ensure the project was actually implemented well.

Included within the initial plan was substantial professional development for the senior leads and those expected to deliver the various elements of the programme. Having identified staff's limited knowledge and their views about literacy as an early problem we needed to ensure it was addressed. Later, significant support was needed for teachers in each subject area to develop approaches to improve pupils' disciplinary literacy. The old adage – if you want it in the classroom, you need it in the staffroom first – is ignored at your peril. Alongside this we built in an evaluation design from the outset. Keeping it simple and straightforward, we wanted to know whether all the work being done was having the desired effect. Balancing this with the overall manageability of data collection, processing and analysing was an on-going challenge.

Finally, a project will not run itself. Certainly not one of this scale. Regular meetings were scheduled with the senior leads to ensure identification of issues at an early stage alongside the half-termly full group meetings. Resolving these issues; keeping people true to the main aspects of the plan; tweaking the plans when necessary; maintaining momentum and focus; and planning events, were all critical to successful implementation. The various meetings also provided different communication channels.

Implementation, in part, involves creating the nodes – structures, systems, processes and practices – associated with improvement. However, successful improvement requires the improvement nodes to be connected by invisible relational bonds, to ensure everything works smoothly and effectively. All improvement work is basically a human endeavour. As Bergman (2018) neatly states, 'Execution is a people problem ...'

Basic 6: Networking

The importance of building and nurturing enriching relationships

The effective leader establishes and maintains productive internal and external relationships. They create the web of invisible bonds that link people together, seeing the person behind the professional persona. While managing change, they ensure a wider perspective on well-being is retained, within and across the organisation.

Summary

- People who work in an organisation bring very different experiences and beliefs to any particular situation or change process. The staff is in fact many different people with a dynamic set of emotions and beliefs that interact in a complex way.
- Specialist knowledge, strategy and high quality implementation all contribute to the change process from a rational and behavioural perspective. It is leaders' social competencies that bring the critical understanding and way of working associated with the emotional element of change. The best leaders are motivation enhancers and multipliers.
- A series of emotional competencies, allied to leadership, were considered learnt rather than innate (Goleman *et al.*, 2002). Highly effective leaders 'typically exhibited a critical mass of strength in a half a dozen or so'. However, the exact combination of skills varied so there was no particular recipe for success.
- Empathy is a critical emotional competency. It was identified as 'the *sine qua non* of all social effectiveness in working life' (Goleman *et al.*, 2002).
- With appropriate reflection, our experiences may help us build greater empathy. However, our experiences are limited.
- People can help us to view things from different perspectives. They can offer different beliefs, values or emphases to the ones we possess, bringing different knowledge and experiences of a variety of contexts.
- As a leader it is too easy to forget, among all your own personal and professional challenges, that some colleagues have difficult and complex lives. All colleagues are likely to go through difficult and complex times. There is a requirement to balance the needs of the individual and the organisation.
- There is a critical need for leaders to see themselves as links within a chain, partnership workers, responsible for the education of all children and young people. Moving from a sense of self, to concern for others – at an organisational and then a system level – is part of a leadership journey towards greater maturity.
- Leadership roles associated less with a position of authority and more with connecting and influencing others are based upon emotional connections. These connections are likely to include a shared sense of purpose and an enriching relationship.
- When out of touch, leaders can create problems for themselves and others that are avoidable. It is developing and utilising more resonant, emotionally intelligent ways of leading that often distinguishes the leaders we are willing to follow from those we just wish to leave.

Networking

When leading change the ability to read people – as individuals, members of a team or as a full staffroom – is critical. Sometimes what has to be done is fixed and other times it may be more open ended, but how a leader chooses to approach a task is invariably within their control. A leader who charges after some future vision, only to turn around and realise that no-one has followed them, will have learnt about leading the hard way. The lack of following may be due to people not aligning with the vision, or too many members of staff may have been left along the way, confused or exhausted, due to a lack of connection, poor communication or excessive workload. Motivating people is no easy feat.

Misquoting Shulman (2004), I would suggest that, 'After 30 years of doing such work, I have concluded that understanding the staffroom and leading people ... is perhaps the most complex, most challenging, and most demanding, subtle, nuanced, and frightening activity that our species has ever invented.'

While leaders, teachers and union representatives may all, at some time, talk about what the staff think and how they are acting or will behave, it is unhelpful to think about the staff as a single entity. People who work in an organisation bring very different experiences and beliefs to a particular situation or change process. The staff is in fact many different people with a dynamic set of emotions and beliefs that interact in a complex way. What a leader has greatest control over, as they seek to influence people, is their own behaviours. These leadership behaviours interact with the behaviours of others, in contexts ranging from relative stability to ones undergoing substantial and significant change, impacting the whole organisation.

Dan and Chip Heath (2010) describe three inter-related aspects of leading change: directing the rider, motivating the elephant, and shaping the path. These are the rational, emotional, and behavioural or habitual elements of the change process. Specialist knowledge, strategy and high quality implementation all contribute to the change process from a rational and behavioural perspective. It is leaders' social competencies that bring the critical understanding and way of working associated with the emotional elements of change.

Emotionally intelligent leaders

'People don't buy what you do, they buy why you do it' (Sinek, 2009). The why and the how operate at an emotional level, they give us a gut feeling about the people who lead us. Later, we may seek to articulate a rationale, based on this gut feeling, about a leader's capabilities. We are more willing to follow people we trust, and we tend to trust people whose values and purpose align with our own and whose actions are in keeping with what they espouse.

We know when we are being led by an inspirational leader but find it difficult to define exactly what it is they do. In *Primal Leadership*, Goleman and colleagues (2002) propose it is not so much what leaders do but how they do it. These leaders create a resonance with others within their organisation, 'They ignite our passion and inspire the best in us', leading to greater individual and collective efforts and ultimately improved performance. We feel empowered. The best leaders are motivation enhancers and multipliers.

'At its root, then, the primal job of leadership is emotional.'

(Goleman *et al.*, 2002)

Goleman and colleagues (2002) proposed a series of emotional competencies allied to leadership. Nine were personal competences, concerned with how we manage ourselves, grouped between self-awareness and self-management. A further ten were classified under social competences; how we manage relationships. These include social awareness (empathy, organisational awareness and service) and relationship management (inspirational leadership, influence, developing others, change catalyst, conflict management, building bonds and teamwork and collaboration).

These emotional intelligence competencies were considered learnt rather than innate. Highly effective leaders 'typically exhibited a critical mass of strength in a half a dozen or so'. However, the exact combination of skills varied so there was no particular recipe for success. Equally effective leaders have very different personalities and personal styles, but there are however some common threads. The most effective leaders often demonstrated a particular strength in at least one of the competencies from each of the four domains.

However, what is striking is the continuous appearance of empathy – 'sensing others' emotions, understanding their perspective and taking an active interest in their concerns' – as a critical emotional competency. It was integral to the four resonant leadership styles (visionary, coaching, affiliative and democratic) and acted as a critical moderator in the two dissonant styles (commanding and pacesetting). Analysing the six leadership styles you can see the importance of the social awareness competency of empathy alongside the relationship management competencies. Empathy was identified as 'the *sine qua non* of all social effectiveness in working life'.

With appropriate reflection, our experiences may help us build greater empathy, but our experiences are limited. Over thirty years of working in schools, I 'failed' at interview on two occasions. The first was an application for a deputy headship. The school hopefully spotted my raw talent or potential, but it was just too raw and this showed up in a few of the responses I gave, in particular one about a critical incident. I led the whole response but failed to actually inform the headteacher! There was a better candidate, one who was more ready and able to take up the position. It would have been a wonderful school to work at and learn from, but it was not to be. The second one was my first interview for headship. Myself and the school were on totally different pages and it would have been a disaster for both parties if I had been appointed.

On both occasions, I had no sense that my failure to secure the job was due to my gender, colour, ethnicity, sexuality or a disability. However, there are many, many people who have experienced bias or discrimination in the recruitment process, generally reflecting other experiences in their lives. While I can understand discrimination at an intellectual level, I have no real experience of it. Hence, I also lack a full appreciation of its emotional impact. I have not felt the anger, frustration or sense of inevitability of a life spent battling societal bias.

It is critical for a leader to see the intellectual, experiential and emotional viewpoints of people as a series of different windows into a person's perspective and behaviours. These must be of importance and interest to leaders. Each of us has a different, possibly even unique hinterland, and we need to be cognisant of the limitations and relative insignificance of the hinterland we possess. We each have a point of view, 'Every viewpoint is a view from a point. We must be able to critique our own perspective if we are to see a fuller truth.' (Rohr, 2020c)

People can help us to view things from a variety of perspectives. They can offer different beliefs, values or emphases to the ones we possess; different knowledge and experiences of a variety of contexts which help enrich decision making. Leaders should strive to improve things at an individual, organisational or societal level. Equality legislation, gender pay gap reporting and the formation of campaigning and support groups – for example, WomenEd and BAMEed – are all potentially transformational responses.

As a leader, it is too easy to forget, among all your own personal and professional challenges, that some colleagues have difficult and complex lives. All colleagues are likely to go through difficult and complex times, and there is a requirement to balance the needs of the individual and the organisation. A teacher not in front of a class or a member of support staff not carrying out their job puts pressure on others, and it is not great for the children and young people to be taught by a succession of different people. It cannot go on for ever. However, failing to support people through difficult times creates an organisation where nobody in their right mind would want to work. It is the act of moving from empathy to a compassionate response that brings the Basic of Networking alive. Our networks consist of the invisible bonds that bind us together. As one of the Ways of Doing, Networking is the summation of the thousands of interactions we have each day, with individuals, with groups, or maybe with the whole organisation. It is important to remember however, that all these interactions are received as if on a one-to-one basis by those we are communicating with.

At the same time as I may be supporting a member of staff who had suffered a bereavement, another member of staff would be experiencing the joy associated with the birth of a new baby. People were getting married, and others were separating or getting divorced. Leading a school with over 100 staff and then an organisation of more than 250, you soon come to appreciate that there is always likely to be a personal issue that needs your attention. There are times people will need to speak to you in confidence about things affecting their lives, as personal events often overspill into work lives. There is a need for leaders to provide people with emotional or practical support, and there is also a need to build the organisational culture and climate to do likewise.

Putting staff first

In *Putting Staff First*, John Tomsett and Jonny Uttley (2020) mapped out 'a blueprint for revitalising our schools'. In the book, their work of the past decade demonstrated a counterbalancing response to the high stakes accountability culture which pervades the education system. They sought to reset the equilibrium position, with a focus on staff's personal well-being, workload reduction, high quality professional development, and a more development related performance management system with an assumption of automatic pay progression. The rationale behind *Putting Staff First* was 'that a healthy, motivated, highly trained, expert staff is the thing which is most likely to help students make good progress in their learning.' It is an application of the principle, 'If you want it in the classroom you need it in the staffroom first'.

Meeting the needs of staff and those of pupils are intertwined supportive strands of a dynamic equilibrium. Staff go the extra mile, and a leader must do so too, whether this means forgetting the rule book on who can or cannot go to a particular funeral or ensuring a parent can go with their child to their first day at school or watch their Christmas play. People have a life outside of school, and sometimes I forgot this as work can become all consuming. The requirement to balance the different needs of different people is a tension that must be managed. Much of the work you do as a leader will be confidential, quiet and unseen. You need to establish a rule of thumb to ensure that when managing different situations for different people, you are reasonable, equitable and balanced.

In *Educating with Purpose*, I described the *telos*, or end point, of the education system as 'a life well lived'. Putting staff first and a life well lived, for children and young people, are the two sides of the coin. Staff are entitled to a life well lived too. Towards the end of the book, I laid down the challenge for our current education system and society in general to create 'A world that will no longer accept a life well lived for the few, but demands it for all.' Part of meeting this challenge is greater empathy and understanding between school leaders.

There is a vital need to move towards a collaborative imperative – seen quite significantly through school leaders' responses to the COVID-19 pandemic – and away from a competitive system that generates winners and losers. Competition, in which we are challenged to be the best version of ourselves we can be and support others to do the same, is powerful and productive. Sadly, too much of the competition we have seen over the decades is of a self-serving or own-school-serving nature. There is a critical need for leaders to see themselves as links within a chain, partnership workers responsible for the education of all children and young people. And as I often say, holding closest to our hearts those children and young people who are most disadvantaged, challenging or vulnerable.

My story, Our story, The story

Moving from a sense of self, to concern for others – at an organisational and then a system level – is part of a leadership journey towards greater maturity. Earlier, I wrote about my three stages of headship. The journey was akin to what is referred to as the cosmic egg, a journey of interconnected domes or layers of increasing maturity (Rohr, 2021). Early headship can often be about establishing yourself, growing into the position of being the leader. This is My story. Behaviours centre on bringing things to the new organisation; 'I did this at my previous school and it really worked' or superimposing your perspective on the organisation. Unfortunately, leaders can get stuck here without ever connecting with a greater meaning or purpose. What worked in one context does not always transfer effectively to another.

Moving to Our story was about my attempts to empower others within the organisation. It was built around a set of processes to move decision making to others and away from me. It was about trusting others and being supportive of their decisions, even when things did not always work out well. This second phase of headship sought to develop empowerment and ownership, engendering a sense of belonging to and growing with the organisation. Again, some leaders get stuck here, defending 'their' organisation and ways of doing things against all comers. Both My story and Our story are necessary parts of understanding ourselves and others but they are not the end of The story.

The story looks at the essence of our humanity and what is universally good and true. It is where a leader looks beyond their school – the staff, children and young people within it – to the greater good of all. This is not necessarily about formal structures. It is perfectly possible for the CEO of a multi-academy trust to be locked in My story and the headteacher of a single school to be immersed in The story, and *vice versa*. The story is about a willingness to act in true partnership. It requires a mindset and desire to act with, through and in support of others. It is accepting that no single leader or organisation has all the solutions to all the problems and challenges we face.

Working with other schools in various partnership arrangements: formally as CEO of a multi-academy trust; as strategic lead of a research school; as the elected chair (often unopposed as no-one else wanted the job) of projects with small to million pounds plus budgets; and in a group like the Headteachers Roundtable, created different ways for me to work with and connect with people. One of most significant leadership differences was the authority to make decisions.

As CEO of a multi-academy trust I was the ultimate decision maker within the remit entrusted to me by the board. In other leadership roles the decision making varied but was always associated less with a position of authority and more with connecting to and influencing others. There is a tendency for less formal or shallower partnerships to fall apart when the communication and emotional connections are weak, and leaders have greater autonomy and an easier opt out. This provides important lessons about ways of leading that are based more upon emotional connections relating to a shared sense of purpose and an enriching relationship, than a formal position of authority. These lessons and ways of working may be utilised even where a leader's authority is connected to their position.

The emotional dimension of leadership is significant and substantial. When out of touch, leaders can create problems for themselves and others that are totally avoidable. They create what Goleman and colleagues (2002) referred to as dissonant leadership; 'needlessly upsetting messages ... resulting in collective distress'. This distress becomes the group's preoccupation and distracts them away from the content of a leader's message and the task in hand or the overall purpose of the organisation, which ultimately leads to poor performance. The resonant leader has the ability to hit just the right notes. The whole group is on the same emotional wavelength and performance is strong. It is developing and utilising these more resonant, emotionally intelligent ways of leading that often distinguishes the leaders we are willing to follow from those we just wish to leave. The Basic of Networking is an essential aspect of leadership.

People impact

As a headteacher and CEO, I actually sorted out relatively few problems, complaints or grievances, most issues were taken care of by other people. However, the ones that tended to land on my desk were the most complex ones. Colleagues bring you problems that have proved difficult to resolve. Sometimes it can be a parent who is not happy until they have seen 'the manager'. I may not have actually done or said anything different to what had gone before, but the parent just accepted it as the final word from the organisation. At other times there was a level of complexity that required my input.

Over time, I developed a way of dealing with the few complex problems that came my way. Meeting with the person to clarify exactly what the concern or complaint was, thereby seeking to understand, is an important first step. This demonstrated that I was dealing with their issue and that their concerns were important to me. I would also ask them what they believed a potential solution might be. This really helps to expose their level of anger. Is the complainant in retributive mode or seeking a just outcome to a perceived error or failure of judgement? I always put the issues and their solution in writing, to check I had fully understood. On a number of occasions, having clarified my understanding and theirs, people would withdraw the complaint. The process provided a perspective that allowed them to look at the issue rationally. Complaints and grievances tend to be emotional responses in the first instance.

When investigating the issue I would make sure the gathering of data was thorough and seen from all viewpoints, as I did not want things to appear later on that I had missed. Sometimes the best way to protect the organisation or individual is by accepting something has gone wrong and then seeking to put it right, but I would never rush to a decision. After considering the evidence carefully, I would again meet with the person, at an agreed pre-arranged time, to explain my decision and follow this up with my determination in writing. I am not Solomon, and I did not always get it right, I just made the best decision I could with the information available. Tending to the emotional dimension of an organisation involves complicated work with individuals and complex work associated with change across the organisation.

An invaluable leadership lesson

Leading change is challenging. People often prefer the status quo rather than the promise of a better future. During times of significant change there is an even greater need for the soft skills associated with people work. When leading change, there is a need to think, in advance, about the likely impact on people. Too often leaders think about what needs to be done and how. Too rarely they think about the emotional dimension of change and the impact on people. Any consideration needs to take account of two factors: the number of people affected and the quantum of the impact. Could business carry on as usual or will there be significant disruption to people's normal working patterns? High emotional impact, what is termed the 'dread factor', would be associated with things like job losses or restructuring as opposed to the lower emotional impact associated with simple changes in working practices or the acquisition of new skills (Oehmen *et al.*, 2018).

In the chapter *Capitalising your assets*, I explained how we used a risk register when forming the multi-academy trust. One risk identified was the need to ensure support staff were receiving equal pay for work of equal value across the three schools, through an equal pay review. Teachers had national terms and conditions, and as such were deemed to already have equal pay for doing work of an equal value.

This review process involved agreeing job descriptions and then using a matrix to score each job against a number of criteria. The total would then be referenced to the appropriate points range which equated to a particular level of pay. The scheme had a rational and objective basis that made it fair and, importantly for employers, defendable if a claim was brought against them. Having completed the process, I was then able to check the new prospective salaries against the current ones, so I was certain no one would lose out as a result of the equal pay review. There was a residual issue around paid holidays for nursery nurses which complicated the outcome, and a few staff who had significant pay rises, but very few. The process had the opportunity for individuals or groups to appeal.

Having completed the rational side of the process, everything seemed in place, but I was not as prepared as I should have been for the emotional dimension that followed. While relatively small, I was genuinely surprised at the number of people who appealed. A few made claims about what they did or were required to do that I would categorise as stretching the truth. Others made pertinent points that were accepted and the point tally was amended accordingly. This sometimes led to a change in pay.

However, what some people were saying through their appeals was 'I do not think this level of salary values what I do or who I am'. I did not disagree with that sentiment then, nor do I now. In many ways the value placed on the job by the salary had become a proxy for their perceived value as a person. The work done by many support staff in public services is significantly undervalued in monetary terms. The COVID-19 pandemic has further identified many other workers, previously unseen within the economy, who matter immensely but suffer the same undervaluing in terms of zero hours contracts and low hourly rates of pay. This is the emotional dimension of change that Dan and Chip Heath (2010) refer to as 'motivating the elephant'. Attempting to stop the emotional elephant from trampling all over planned changes requires work at both a personal and organisational level. Good communication is part of this as long as the emotional dimension is considered.

Communicating with people and the person

I think it was an army general who used to ask his subordinate officers, 'How much did you communicate with your team last week?' No matter what answer they gave him, he always responded that it was not enough. The amount of communication we do matters but also the type and way we communicate. In the *Salesperson's Secret Code*, (Mills *et al.*, 2017), the authors identify what they term destination beliefs, one of which is communication. There are two very different beliefs about successful communication, described in the book as journey motivators:

- Journey motivator 1 – Great communication is about getting your message across clearly and succinctly (lightning) – communication is all about the great pitch or presentation.
- Journey motivator 2 – Great communication is all about creating deep and meaningful dialogue (thunder) – communication is about forming, building and sustaining relationships.

The analogy of thunder and lightning is both powerful and useful. Too often leaders get caught up trying to fire multiple lightning bolts to communicate a rationale or intellectual aspect of change. There is a need and a place for that style of communication, but it is often overused. What is often required is more rumbling thunder, constituting 'deep and meaningful dialogue ... building and sustaining relationships'. The rumbling thunder may happen in the staffroom at breaktime or lunch, when out and about on corridors, and by keeping an open door policy. There are also more structural responses associated with the dialogue engendered when coaching is built into new developments or leaders seek feedback about the organisation on a regular basis. Rolling thunder is integral to the Basic of Networking because it uses meaningful dialogue to build and sustain relationships.

When I first became a headteacher in 2000, I sat down with every member of staff for a twenty-minute conversation around a few generic questions based on what the school did well, and what it needed to improve. Two issues came up repeatedly; that the senior leadership team was dysfunctional, and that printing was a nightmare. The printing was sorted overnight with a part-time, term time only appointment, and this bought me massive leadership capital; 'We were listened to, and our concerns were acted on'. Developing the leadership team took longer but was a key part of the work I did early on in headship. The most important thing, however, was that I sat down and spoke with every member of staff. It was the base from which relationships were built. As a leader, never underestimate the gratitude people feel when you give them time.

From the end of that very first year, I always conducted an annual staff evaluation of the year. The questions were pretty standard, and staff responded on a scale from one to ten. Just about every year and for every question someone would give a score of one and someone else a score of ten. Before the end of term, I would send out the mean score for each question and a list of positive changes and backwards steps that appeared on ten percent or more of responses. At the start of the new academic year, I would return to the staff evaluation and the issues identified with proposals about how they would be addressed. This process, with its feedback loop to staff, was part of building dialogue, trust and ultimately relationships.

This type of process is useful in a number of ways. Firstly, while it does not provide a laser-like evaluation of specific issues, it does gives you a feel for the organisation. Secondly, it can get any angst out in the open. All organisations have their shadow sides, the dark places in which equally dark conversations may be going on. Sometimes it is better to get these out into the open and start to address them. It is all part of working on, and with, the emotional elements present in all organisations.

Positive relationships formed with members of staff are important and can be usefully deepened as you write and implement policies. In 2014, as we were forming the multi-academy trust, the *School Teachers' Pay and Conditions Document* (STPCD) included annual performance pay for the first time. The proposals caused a lot of anxiety, and a number of younger teachers, with hefty university debts, were particularly concerned. Again, I had not realised. It had never crossed my mind that they would not progress annually up the pay spine.

An open invitation, voluntary group – including union representatives – was formed to look at the issue. It came up with a proposal for automatic pay progression for three years with a performance related pay bar after M3 on the main scale. The proposal was adopted. The informal strategy and engagement of staff, who doubtless went back and relayed the discussions and proposals to colleagues, made the formal adoption of the process very easy. A few years later, we just went for automatic progression for the full main scale for teachers; that is, no performance related pay. It is one of a number of decisions that have helped ensure very healthy retention rates among teaching staff.

Communication tools and tactics need to be used within a wider authentic dialogical approach that strengthens and deepens relationships. This enables the discretionary effort and goodwill that all schools rely on to achieve good outcomes for the children and young people they serve. It is equally important not to allow this discretionary effort to be wasted on tasks of relatively low importance. Jerrim, Sims and Allen (2021) identified 'two clear areas where reducing teachers' workloads would likely reduce stress: lesson preparation and marking.' The case for spending less time on marking was explicitly made. Unsurprisingly, supportive leadership and manageable workloads were two key factors in controlling workplace stress levels. School leaders were also called upon to involve 'teachers in decision making processes, supporting their professional development and explicitly recognising staff for their work.'

Bring your best and worst marking

Policies are great on paper but getting them to work in the staffroom and classroom can be problematic. Even when a policy launch is smooth and successful there is a need to revisit, refine and reconsider. Too often policies are launched and then another policy is launched and then another. Time to refine the policy and develop staff is simply not given, and consequently moving the words from the page into embedded practice does not happen. Taking an alternative approach, writing policy on the basis of the best observable practice, that is, practice which has a positive impact on pupils' learning, is about identifying sustainable, real world exemplary practice and helping all teachers consistently develop similar appropriate practice. It is about utilising the professional staff community in wisdom building.

Increasing the ability of each teacher to use good professional judgement to decide what and how to mark, alongside other beneficial activities including lesson planning, developing schemes of learning, or working on a particular aspect of their practice, is at the core of wisdom building. The process is slower but potentially goes deeper and has a long lasting impact on outcomes. The strength of any process like this is the dialogue which is developed. Moving from policy to practice includes setting the expectation and monitoring to ensure compliance. In some life and death or high risk activities this is a sound approach. Marking books is neither a matter of life and death nor a high risk activity. Hence it is reasonable to adopt an approach of moving the opposite way, from practice to policy.

In 2014 National Curriculum levels were about to disappear. The data wave was at its highest and like most schools, we were being overwhelmed by data and marking. Various marking policies had been implemented, but they had largely served as workload multipliers. While there is a need to mark pupils' work, the challenge is how, how much and to what extent an individual teacher should decide versus a school or departmental policy.

By 2012 I had received my third successive Ofsted report as a headteacher that had identified the need to improve the volume, quality and consistency of marking, as a key issue for improvement. We attempted to implement six data drops per year. Each data drop had a marking scrutiny associated with it. We never managed the six data drops or marking scrutinies due to a late Easter and a very short half term. We actually managed five data drops that year; four the following year, and eventually dropped to two. The marking scrutiny with samples of books passed to middle leaders and then senior leaders was time consuming, stressful and of limited value. The same may be said of the four or five data drops.

As an alternative, teachers were asked to bring their best and worst examples of marking to a meeting. It was to be a different type of marking scrutiny. Looking at a small self-selected sample of best practice lowers the emotional challenge to an individual. However, the worry of whether your colleagues will agree with your thoughts on best practice and the requirement to bring your worst marking and show it off in public may act as a rather weighty counterbalance. Looking at it simplistically, if a teacher marks six books to bring along to the discussion and has not marked any other books all year, this process will not reveal it. In the short term, this approach will not ensure consistent marking of all books. The system is predicated on trust, and this kind of leadership approach is a long-term, slow burn approach to school improvement. It is important to understand the difference between policy to practice versus practice to policy approaches.

Informing experience and practice with research added to our depth of understanding as we looked to limit marking to that which would have impact on pupils' learning. That is, it is worth the time invested. Guiding the discussion so people think deeply about what they are doing, getting people to challenge their own practice – affirming what is useful and identifying what is unnecessary – requires a coaching style approach. Listening to staff talk and looking at the evidence led to us agreeing some key points:

- That teacher comments with no response from a pupil were of no value.
- To reduce the number of codes used to correct literacy errors. Many were never used, and others used inconsistently.
- To stop the practice of excessive photographing and sticking evidence in books. While it looked pretty, it did not aid learning. A single picture annotated by the child was of more value.
- To use numbered success criteria and yellow box marking where appropriate. Teachers were stopped from writing the same success criteria multiple times across a whole class set of books. The idea of re-teaching common class errors gained traction.

These changes look very dated now but at the time of implementation were a massive step forward.

Our original marking policy and associated monitoring processes were symptomatic of the prevailing high surveillance, low trust monitoring culture found in schools at that time. It was a monitoring culture focused on checks after the event, just in case an inspector called. Too little of this work had a positive impact on the quality of education of children and young people, and too much of it had a negative impact on the well-being and development of teachers.

Accountability can be an integral part of improving an organisation. It has a part to play but must be held in balance with the emotional impact on the organisation. Fear is a poor long-term motivator, rather it is important to focus on the resourcefulness and potential of all the humans working within the organisation. The realisation of this potential is obviously supported through developing expertise but also forms part of the three foci of Guardianship, one of the Basics constituting the Way of Doing.

Basic 7: Guardianship

The importance of a low stakes, high trust improvement-focused culture

The effective leader sets and maintains the standards expected of, and met within, the organisation. They understand the potential and limitations of the different accountability tools at their disposal. Maintaining a high trust culture, their primary response to any conclusions reached is focused on improvement rather than consequences.

Summary

- All organisations and systems require an appropriate, meaningful and effective set of checks and balances.
- Accountability systems involve assessments, the collection and analysis of data and information, the formation of judgements and conclusions, and ultimately actions. Any system will contain a series of compromises.
- Time spent on assessment or accountability has to be balanced and in proportion to its intended use. Limiting the time spent on assessment may lower the reliability. As such any judgements made should be more circumspect and provisional.
- The inspection system is in essence an inquiry-based model. This model has in-built limitations and relatively high unreliability. It would be preferable and more honest for inspectors to make judgements and record them as a nuanced narrative as opposed to a definitive number.
- In considering data, leaders need to appreciate what conclusions may and may not be drawn from a particular data set. Validity is a concept linked to conclusions drawn.
- Leaders need to choose wisely from the different accountability tools available. Various tools, with different uses, strengths and limitations exist, including assessing standards (inspection or evaluation), assuring quality (audit), and responsive leadership (feedback loops).
- There is a danger in education that we believe everything we implement has a positive impact. This happens because we continually fail to evaluate what we do.
- Assuring standards can be used more formatively through building an appropriate level of evaluation into improvement cycles. Alongside audit and feedback loops, these three processes sit at the heart of a self-improving school system.
- A focus on improvement can be exciting, engaging and on occasion all-consuming, as it is often driven by a moral purpose. It encourages people to take responsibility and gives them a sense of being able to respond. They have a level of control over events and how the organisation may be improved.
- Part of assuring high standards is building and sustaining the systems and processes that are most likely to achieve them. These systems and processes are what leaders have greatest control over. Simplicity, consistency and stability are all key.
- Leaders can learn about the effectiveness of improvement efforts using a process of questioning, interpreting and responding. It is what I term responsive leadership.

Guardianship

All organisations and systems require an appropriate, meaningful and effective set of checks and balances. Setting the standards expected is the easier part. Ensuring they are upheld – on a cold, windy, miserable day in the middle of November with the rain coming in horizontally from the Irish Sea – is the greater challenge. Ensuring high standards is the fundamental purpose of the Basic of Guardianship. High standards in theory are not the problem; the rhetoric easily rolls off the tongue. High standards in practice are more of a challenge.

In part this is due to people having different views on which standards need to be included in any assessment, how best to assess them and to what extent there is a hierarchy within the standards assessed or available. Accountability and an organisation's purpose and moral compass are inextricably linked. What matters most, raw attainment or progress? Should progress be contextualised when looking at the impact of schools with very different intakes? What level of tolerance, if any, should be given where a school's behaviour or admissions systems deliberately or inadvertently leads to greater exclusion or less inclusion of groups of pupils who tend to perform less well? To what extent should the interplay between different standards be taken into account?

Accountability systems have at their core a set of processes that involve assessments, the collection and analysis of data or information, the formation of judgements or conclusions, and ultimately actions. A system will contain a series of compromises. The reliability of assessments may generally be improved by increasing their length. This enables all the important elements associated with a particular construct to be measured. However, time spent on assessment, and the related processes, has to be balanced and in proportion to the intended use.

Limiting the time spent on assessment may lower the reliability. Observing a teacher for one to three hours over the course of a year, when their total teaching time is likely to be eight to nine hundred hours, is one such example. In this example, we would want to be extremely circumspect and provisional in any judgements made. Unfortunately, that is not how the system or the lesson grading observation process – adopted from Ofsted's inspection system – works. Despite the limited data and significant reliability issues related to the amount of time spent observing the teacher, the involvement of a single assessor, the absence of an agreed reliable lesson observation assessment rubric, limited or no training for the assessor, and different views on what actually constitutes good teaching, cliff edged grading judgements continue to be made by too many school leaders.

The high stakes inspection system has existed in the English education system for over two decades. It has had a detrimental impact on the development of balanced accountability systems within schools and across the system. Stripping back the inspection system, it is in essence an inquiry-based model which has in-built limitations and relatively high unreliability. Yet this is not taken into account in the cliff edged reporting system. No inspection report has ever given a school one of the four grades available with the associated confidence interval. Arguably, if we continue grading schools, reports should read something like this, 'This school is graded 2, it is a good school, and we are confident that it sits somewhere in the range 1-3 (outstanding to requires improvement). The inspectors are reasonably confident it is not inadequate'.

To address these reliability issues, the inspection process could be significantly extended to involve multiple visits from different teams over a number of years before any attempt was made to grade a school. However, this is not a good use of the limited public funding available for education, or school leaders' time. It would be preferable and more honest for inspectors to make judgements and record them in a nuanced narrative as opposed to a definitive number. By more honest, I mean that the conclusion drawn is in keeping with the limitations of the process, information and data available.

In considering data, inspectors and school leaders need to appreciate what conclusions may and may not be drawn from a particular data set. The General Certificate of Secondary Education (GCSE) is a reliable assessment from which to draw conclusions about the amount of knowledge pupils have of a certain subject, but it is not perfect. No set of GCSE examinations assess the total content contained within the syllabus, and there will be differences in the judgements made between markers assessing the papers. Despite these issues, it is a reliable assessment on which to draw conclusions about a pupil's knowledge of a subject. It is, however, a pretty poor measure on which to draw conclusions about the effectiveness of a school. Validity is a concept linked to conclusions drawn. A pupil's GCSE grade is impacted by a whole series of issues, including gender, ethnicity, parental support and socio-economic status. This means that using GCSEs – or other similar assessments at various stages during a child's time at school – to judge school effectiveness fails to take into account important aspects associated with a school's effectiveness. The GCSE assessment is still reliable but the conclusions being drawn about school effectiveness are not valid.

An understanding of reliability and validity is important when determining how best to use accountability within an organisation, as well as across a system. There is a need to choose wisely from the different accountability tools available. Various tools, with different uses, strengths and limitations exist, including assessing standards (inspection or evaluation), assuring quality (audit), and responsive leadership (feedback loops). The first has been excessively pursued through the accountability system for the past two decades. Assessing standards through inspection is akin to a post-mortem, in that it occurs after the event and attempts to look back and learn lessons. It has no impact in real time. Instead of this more summative approach, assuring standards can be used more formatively, and involves building an appropriate level of evaluation into improvement cycles. Evaluation as a process is significantly underutilised. Alongside the two latter tools, this is at the heart of a self-improving school system.

Evaluation by design

There is a danger in education that we believe everything we implement has a positive impact. This happens because we continually fail to evaluate what we do. From Government to school leaders to teachers, in the absence of any evidence, we conclude a particular intervention or initiative had a positive impact, simply on the basis that we did it. Over the years, I have listened to and read pieces, for example by Professors Becky Allen (2019), Rob Coe (2014) and Dylan Wiliam (2018) who, using empirical research, have systematically pulled apart many of the strongly held beliefs or political fads associated with school improvement. From grading lessons to excessive use of data, performance pay, teacher recruitment, curriculum reform and academisation, all have varying and limited impact on school and system-wide improvement.

From the evidence or research informed movement's early days of certainty – with people playing researcher top trumps … 'Yes, but Professor X says …' – we are starting to see greater nuance and sophistication in people's understanding. Laboratory-based research deliberately seeks to isolate and control variables. Researchers seek to simplify the system to understand impact, interactions and causation. The classroom environment is inherently complex.

There is now an increasing acceptance that even where the research is less ambiguous, implementation in different classrooms, with their different teachers and pupils, often does not replicate the initial laboratory-based research. This seems to be even more pronounced when there are attempts to scale particular interventions. Experts appear willing to embrace uncertainty, and leaders may also wish to tread more gently and speak with less certainty. A school leader does not have the luxury of being able to wait for more research, and only addressing an issue when there is certainty of the way forward. As a leader, deciding whether to act or not to act has implications for pupils, staff, parents and the wider community. Where there is an issue to be resolved and a signpost as to the way forward, it may be best to trial an approach, then assess and evaluate before moving to a larger scale.

A leader may not have the expert knowledge of evaluation processes possessed by professional researchers, but leaders do need to develop an enhanced knowledge. An evaluation process is required to look critically at improvement projects and initiatives. This requires a change in focus from 'data for the purpose of inspection to data for the purpose of learning' (Heath, 2020). The former is focused on consequences for the individual or organisation whereas the latter is focused on improvement. A focus on improvement can be exciting, engaging and on occasion all-consuming, as it is often driven by a moral purpose. It encourages people to take responsibility and gives them a sense of being able to respond. They have a level of control over events and how the organisation may be improved.

In planning the Key Stage 3 literacy project across Blackpool we built in evaluation from the outset. It involved a number of standardised assessment tests, an attitudinal survey, and a series of case studies. One of the standardised assessments chosen was the New Group Reading Test (NGRT) from GL Assessment, an assessment taken by over 100,000 pupils each year. It was appropriate for our purpose of assessing a pupil's ability to read. It also allowed us to compare the standard and progress of our pupils against a national cohort. There were a number of different analyses including sentence completion (associated with word recognition and use) and passage comprehension abilities. The first set of NGRT data was stark. It showed that 10% of pupils in Key Stage 3 in Blackpool schools were in the lowest stanine (Stanine 1). This is two and a half times the national average. In Educational Diversity, a Pupil Referral Unit, 31% of pupils were in the lowest stanine. That is a very large percentage of pupils who will struggle to access the curriculum, and up to this point, the scale of the issue across Blackpool had not been grasped.

A working hypothesis was that many of the problems encountered in reading linked back to unmet speech and language needs. So, as well as the more universal reading programme and associated specific interventions, it was clear that a bespoke plan for what became known as the 'Stanine 1 and 2 issue' would be needed. This is an example of the importance of assessing standards as part of a formative rather than a summative approach. It shifts the emphasis from a post-mortem, after the event analysis, to a more dynamic real time investigative approach that impacts more explicitly on the improvement journey.

In a similar vein, the data at the end of the first year of the project was interesting. For pupils in Years 7 and 9, the NGRT average standard age score showed an increase in four of the eight schools ranging between three to five points. In three other academies the NGRT average standard age score was identical to the baseline score at the beginning of the year. It would not be totally unreasonable to suggest that in these schools the project had little impact. However, in the last academy involved, the score dropped six points. From careful project monitoring and discussions, we knew that this final academy had struggled to retain a senior project lead, with the result that implementation was pretty much non-existent. Of all the changes to staffing we experienced during the programme, it was the changes to senior staff that had greatest impact. Each time a school changed their senior leaders a new person had to get up to speed without the benefit of the previously held training and the experience of involvement in the literacy programme.

There is now a small but discernible correlation in the NGRT data between the schools that have been able to maintain the same leader throughout the programme and those where this has not been possible. This is not evidence of causation but is part of the data that school leaders would need to be cognisant of when leading major school improvement processes. The data is more a signpost towards, or suggestion of, what might be of significance and worthy of noting. It is not definitive, but it appears that stability in project leadership matters.

I may just be suffering from IKEA or self-service bias, but I wonder whether the six-point drop in the standard age scores in the final academy was representative of what normally happened in Blackpool schools – or more generally – to disadvantaged pupils. The divergence in NGRT standard age scores between disadvantaged pupils and their more advantaged peers – possibly indicative of literacy more generally – mirrors the difference seen at GCSE. This would suggest that not only the four academies where positive progress was made, but also the three where the NGRT standard age scores had not declined, could be seen as having achieved positive outcomes.

The Basic of Guardianship involves assuring high standards through the building and sustaining of the appropriate systems and processes most likely to achieve them. These systems and processes are what leaders have greatest control over. Simplicity, consistency and stability are all key. It is important that the systems and processes which form the operational backbone of an organisation's success, can be sustained with relative ease. This allows leaders the time and the critical head space, or capacity within working memory, to engage both with the demands of the moment and with more strategic thoughts and actions. Throughout any evaluation process, assessing standards must be about finding ways to improve. It is not about apportioning blame and consequences for individuals or schools.

Responsive leadership

All teachers will be familiar with formative assessment or responsive teaching. One aspect involves teachers asking quality questions, interpreting the answers or information given, and appropriately responding in real time to improve the learning of pupils. Using a similar process of questioning, interpreting and responding, leaders can learn about the on-going impact of planned improvements and the actions required to keep them on track. It is what I term responsive leadership and involves the creation of feedback loops.

In *Upstream*, Heath (2020) describes attempts to improve the education system, 'We could try to concoct the perfect intervention – the new curriculum, the new model – and hope for the best. Or we could settle for a pretty good solution that's equipped with so many feedback loops it can't help but get better over time. The second option is the one that system thinkers would endorse'. The genius of leaders is not just in their knowledge of the various accountability tools. It is in their ability to select the most appropriate tool for the matter in hand and their willingness to respond effectively to the data and information obtained. Leaders need to explicitly create feedback loops in important systems, processes and developments and respond to the data and information they provide.

As part of the Key Stage 3 literacy project, in Autumn Term 2019, Alex Quigley devised a survey to gain the views of school staff using eleven questions. Alex worked with the project as the literacy specialist and critical friend. The survey was divided into three different sections:

- Questions 1 - 4 looked at self-efficacy and beliefs. This was to understand whether there had been a change in beliefs, knowledge or practice at teacher level.
- Questions 5 - 7 looked at school prioritisation of literacy. This was to understand whether schools had made visible changes in prioritising literacy.
- Questions 8 - 11 looked at professional development and implementation. This was to understand whether there were the systems and structures in place to make change happen in schools, including at a subject level.

Respondents were asked to answer strongly agree, agree, undecided, disagree, or strongly disagree, to each of the eleven statements. A final question gave the opportunity for a more open response about future requirements for developing the explicit teaching of literacy. Information about the respondents' role and subject responsibility was also collected for analysis purposes. There were over three hundred responses from staff across the eight schools involved to the first survey, and just under three hundred to the follow up one a year later.

The staff surveys showed there were high levels of consensus across subjects and layers of leadership around self-efficacy and beliefs, and the extent to which schools were prioritising literacy. The percentages of strongly agree or agree from respondents were 90.9% and 91.6% respectively. However, there was a significant drop in relation to the professional development and implementation to support the embedding of literacy, where the strongly agree or agree response was only 61.9%. The average hid stark differences in the perception of senior leaders (86.6%) compared to middle leaders (60.6%), and even lower were the classroom teachers – tasked with delivering disciplinary literacy – with just 54.3% strongly agreeing or agreeing with the statements about professional development and implementation of literacy.

The top three 'asks' from staff were for more time for departmental planning, specific training and resources, and additional professional development on disciplinary literacy. As a consequence, the following year there was significant investment in the training of the senior leads and subject leaders in bespoke disciplinary literacy approaches and specific tools. This led to an increase in the strongly agree or agree responses in the following year's staff survey from 61.9% to 72%, for questions nine to eleven on professional development and implementation.

The creation of these feedback loops and the response of leaders is a crucial part of the improvement process, and helps keep the stakes low. Where the stakes are high there is a danger, through fear or choice, that people attempt to subvert measures, including through unethical behaviours. Keeping the stakes low is part of a cultural approach to accountability within an organisation, and involves systems that seek to build responsibility across the organisation. Senior leaders must create systems and processes that actively engage middle leaders and teachers in the accountability processes.

First do no harm

The first maxim of any accountability system must be *primum non nocere* (first do no harm). The dangers of our high stakes accountability system, with a primary focus on summative inspection, are seen in the unintended and unwanted consequences it produces. The current accountability system is damaging the schools who are already the most fragile; those serving the most disadvantaged communities. In June 2018, I published *Graphically Exposing Ofsted Bias?* The blog was based on a series of graphs provided to a headteacher by Ofsted's schools' data and analysis team. The headteacher was fearful of taking it any further as his school was 'in the window'. Over the following days I was contacted by Ofsted's data team and then their public relations team. I have never publicly shared this before but in the original email from Ofsted's schools' data and analysis team the analyst stated, 'Initial signs are that it is going to show something interesting, so thanks for suggesting it!' Ofsted's public relations team took a very different view and closed ranks. Burying its head in the sand, Ofsted failed to address a fundamental flaw in its inspection process.

The graphs provided were a slight variation on the ones normally used by Ofsted, and used eligibility for free school meals (FSM) rather than the geographically based IDACI measure. Using free school meals allowed analysis at a pupil level based on different characteristics including ethnicity. Schools were grouped into quintiles in the graphs. The first thing to note was a stark difference between Ofsted's judgements in primary and secondary schools. While 81% of primary schools in the most deprived quintile were judged to be 'good' or 'outstanding', the figure plummeted to 64% for secondary schools. Looking solely at the secondary school data, the inspection grades were re-organised into quintiles based on the percentage of pupils that were white British and eligible for free school meals, in each school. The percentage range of FSM for each quintile is given next to the number of schools in each quintile on the graph below. An obvious pattern appears.

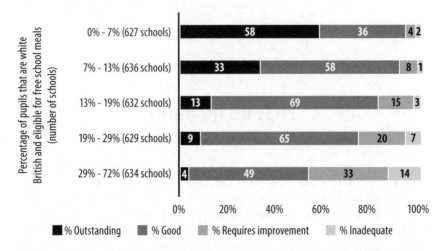

Working in the most deprived quintile, with a high proportion of disadvantaged white British pupils, means you are statistically far more likely to be graded as 'requires improvement' or 'inadequate', and far less likely to be graded 'outstanding'. In fact, nearly half of the schools in the most deprived quintile were graded 'inadequate' or 'requires improvement' compared to just 6% of schools in the least deprived quintile. The difference in outstanding grades awarded is simply outrageous; 4% in the most deprived quintile compared to 58% in the least deprived.

More schools in the most deprived areas are put into a negative spiral by the statistically more likely adverse Ofsted inspection judgement. This may lead to naming and shaming with more teachers leaving both the school and the profession (Worth, De Lazzari and Hillary, 2017). There may also be a loss of confidence in the school by parents, pupils and the local community, with consequences for pupil numbers and budgets. A conveyor belt approach of trying to satisfy a series of Ofsted monitoring visits with a variety of short-term fixes ensues. These schools are being held accountable for a problem that society has failed to resolve. The problem that needs to be addressed is poverty.

While inspection is a human business it is not a humane one. It suffers from two related issues in its inspection of schools in the most challenging circumstances, a lack of proximity to the problems, and increasingly organisational blindness (terms taken from Heath, 2020).

Due to the criteria Ofsted use to appoint inspectors, an inspector is far more likely to come from a school with an intake that has high prior attainment or is more affluent. These inspectors may have met, in their careers, the impact on children and families of domestic violence, poor mental health, substance abuse, homelessness, poor living conditions, insufficient food to eat or energy to heat the home, neglect, and other forms of abuse. However, too many inspectors are unlikely to have met these issues at the quantum seen in the most deprived and disadvantaged areas. To fully understand the complexity of leading a school where there is a profound depth and density of disadvantage you need to experience it.

Inspectors' lack of proximity leads to limited understanding and consequentially the inability to contextualise the exceptional work done by many schools serving the most disadvantaged communities. This was once again brought to the fore when Her Majesty's Chief Inspector criticised schools who prioritised 'making food parcels' and 'going out visiting' disadvantaged children, over delivering remote learning during the first wave of the pandemic (Gibbons, 2021). The 'visiting' was a crucial part of many schools' response to ensure the safeguarding of children and young people. The provision of food parcels was a necessary humanitarian response. The comments were clumsy; rooted in an ignorance of working in and with our most disadvantaged communities.

The latest iteration of the *Education Inspection Framework* promised to 'reward schools in challenging circumstances'. However, a year after its launch, Ofsted admitted that schools with the most deprived intakes are still less likely to be judged 'good' (Allen-Kinross, 2019). Despite being inspected for over two decades, it is little wonder that we have over four hundred schools that have been described by Ofsted as stuck, with persistently low standards. The inspection process is not helping these schools improve. In fact, it seems to be doing more harm than good.

Heath (2020) makes the point that, 'Every system is perfectly designed to get the results it gets'. Ofsted's system is designed to downgrade schools serving the greatest number of vulnerable children and young people; it chooses what to measure, how to measure, and who will measure. The inspectorate appears to be making conclusions about schools' effectiveness while being blind to huge differences in pupil intake.

Unfortunately, the English education system has become addicted to an accountability system based on high stakes consequences. Increasingly, it is blind to the limitations of the current inspection tool used and the alternative accountability tools available. These limitations led to the Headteachers' Roundtable – a group of headteachers who operate as a policy think tank – proposing that it was time to #PauseOfsted. The challenge was laid down to school leaders who operated as Ofsted inspectors to stop enabling the flawed system. With so much of the inspectorate made up of leaders employed by schools, the profession had the collective power to pause and then replace the current inspection process with a better one. Less than six weeks after the Headteachers' Roundtable's call, at their annual summit in February 2020, all Ofsted inspections ceased. However, this was due to the COVID-19 pandemic rather than the group's campaign.

Ofsted has the potential to be an effective part of the accountability system, but it is currently too powerful, insufficiently accountable and over-using the inspection process. The failure to consider other accountability tools is damaging, and nowhere more so than in the area of safeguarding children and young people. An after-the-event quality control process has too often failed those who should have been protected. Safeguarding is weak at a system level and recent events have exposed significant and substantial organisational issues.

The need for a reset

The disturbing statements on the *Everyone's Invited* website show the systemic nature of sexual harassment and abuse suffered overwhelmingly by girls and young women in the education system. It is likely that pupils in all schools and universities have been affected by these issues. The accountability system needs to provide maximum assurance that safeguarding structures and processes will keep children and young people safe.

Ofsted has been the system regulator while this harassment and abuse has been occurring. The inspectorate has failed to either identify the issue or address it over the decades. In part this is due to the very limited priority given to safeguarding during the standard inspection process. The once every three or more years inspection process lacks the agility and regularity to effectively ensure the safety of our young people. A post-mortem after the event is too late. In short, inspection is the wrong tool for the job. Safeguarding is an audit rather than an inspection issue.

In 2016, the Headteachers' Roundtable proposed the formation of an Institute of Chartered Safeguarding Officers (ICSO); akin to the Institute of Chartered Accountants of England and Wales. The ICSO would be responsible for the training, accreditation, and maintenance of a register of chartered safeguarding officers. These chartered safeguarding officers would be responsible for conducting termly safeguarding audits in schools as part of an on-going iterative audit-response-audit system. This would include directly reporting to a governing body or Trust board who would be required to respond to any issues identified. This approach would lead to a substantial strengthening of safeguarding. If we are to address and effectively deal with harassment and abuse in all its forms, I believe the investment in establishing such a system would be beneficial for decades to come.

Governance and quality assurance

To support high quality governance when I was CEO of the Trust, we developed a number of quality assurance (audit) frameworks. The safeguarding framework had a series of actions which occurred on an annual basis: checking policy compliance; an externally conducted safeguarding audit; and implementation and monitoring of any audit recommendations. Myself or the headteachers were responsible for ensuring these were actioned, with the directors' ethos and community committee monitoring the process and outcomes.

In addition, there were actions conducted on a termly basis by the headteachers: completing a single central record check and rectifying any omissions; ensuring the designated safeguard lead and deputy had up-to-date training at the required level; and ensuring that there was a secure central record of all child protection cases and information. I monitored these actions to ensure they were done in a timely manner. In addition, there was a section that covered attendance, persistent absences, and exclusions. Headteachers reviewed these aspects weekly with their senior teams, and I discussed the data with them half termly. All these data sets were reported and discussed with directors on a termly basis, but by the time discussions with directors occurred, each of the schools had already reacted and responded to issues, close in time to the point of first identification.

Central to the safeguarding quality assurance process was an annual externally led safeguarding audit. We asked Blackpool Council to conduct these audits on behalf of the Trust. The first set of external audits occurred in June 2015 and a RAG (Red – Amber – Green) rated report was produced for each academy and submitted to directors. The process involved two different sets of personnel from Blackpool. One group looked at administrative arrangements associated with policies and procedures, management responsibilities, monitoring and evaluation, recruitment and selection of staff, and training and support. The evidence used here was largely paper based. The other group focused on the school's involvement with children, families and external partners, the safety of the school environment, identification, assessment and referral of issues, information sharing, confidentiality and record keeping, and curriculum and learning. This group gained its evidence from discussions with staff and pupils. The process evolved over the years, moving to look at the safeguarding culture within the academies.

There were a number of other elements to the quality assurance frameworks. Barry Leyland, the Chair of the board, produced a simple one page document consisting of a table with a list of policies down the left-hand side and Autumn, Spring, and Summer term, dated for the next five years, along the top. The particular term that each policy would be required to be written or reviewed was highlighted. The page was printed off and put on the noticeboard in my office.

Some policies were annual, often requiring writing or updating in the Autumn term, such as the academies' financial regulations, admissions policy, committee terms of reference, pay policy (teachers), register of business interests, and the directors' report on SEN. Others were part of a two or three year review and update cycle, for example human relationships and sex education (HRSE) policy, supporting pupils with medical conditions, appraisal policy for support staff, capability procedures, charging and remissions policy, discipline policy for staff, flexible working policy, managing staff sickness absence procedures, personal and special leave guidance for staff, staffing establishment (redundancy procedures), whistleblowing policy, professional development and appraisal policy for teachers and support staff, and the grievance policy.

Looking at the term ahead, I would manage the writing and reviewing of policies, consulting as required. This is not work that fuels a leader's passion for the job, but it is a necessary part of it. Each term, I would tick off the policies as they went to the relevant meeting and add new policies if required. Each September, it was a five-minute job to roll everything forward twelve months and then add the table to the Trust's business plan. On occasion there may be an agreed delay in producing a policy, for example, we were waiting for an update of the Diocesan HRSE Diocesan Policy, or when key safeguarding directives from the Department for Education did not align with our calendar. The policies tick list on my noticeboard allowed for the easy management of the policies and documentation required. The policies calendar I left my successor went up to the Summer term of 2024.

Alongside the policies calendar, I produced an annual quality assurance framework to help align the work of the senior leaders with that of the directors. It chimed with the rhythm of the school year, with a month-by-month identification of what was required to ensure the systems and processes that governed organisational life were maintained. Again, it was printed off and put on my wall with items ticked off as they were completed. With the months of the year, from September to July, across the top of the table, we identified the key components of systems and processes that would need to be maintained, grouping them as follows:

- Education – Academic standards, attendance and behaviour, professional development, safeguarding, and ethos.
- Business functions – Governance, finance, health and safety, professional development, and safeguarding.

Each month I would look at the next few months ahead, identifying what I needed to have on my 'to do' list and for when. This included items that would need to be discussed at meetings prior to being actioned. Being organised is a key enabler of effective leadership. I discussed this in more detail in the Basic of Introspection.

Over the years there was an on-going shift, in the Trust's monitoring and accountability systems, towards a more formative, improvement-focused view of accountability. These systems consisted of what I would term high trust, low stakes, developmental processes like the quality assurance system explained above. Another such example was how we reviewed aspects of the curriculum.

Bring the best and worst of your curriculum plans

As previously shared, the Trust's strategic development plan largely consisted of objectives focused on improving the focus, continuity and sequencing of the curriculum from Early Years to Sixth Form. There was an agreed planning format based on learning across a unit of work. There had been a considerable initial investment in the professional development of staff, which was aimed at ensuring they understood the elements of the planning format, and more importantly, why these elements were important. Over the years considerable time was given to departments and phases to collaboratively plan their curriculums, which included Inset days as well as regular meeting time during the year. Using the 'best and worst marking' format, subject leads were invited to bring their best and worst schemes of work to a meeting involving myself, the headteacher and the senior line manager. The brief was fairly simple; talk about your best and worst schemes of learning.

In these meetings, I was sat with a bit of paper with a list of the key components of the planning process: identification of the big ideas, concepts or laws pupils were to learn and any common misconceptions; the core knowledge pupils would need to retain (*stickability*); how assessment would be used to support teaching and learning; the structure of the knowledge in the unit, habits of mind or procedural knowledge and the learner attributes that would be developed (metacognition); and finally the flow or sequence of what was to be taught. The meetings all started the same way. The middle leader was simply asked to explain why they considered the two documents to represent the best and the worst of their schemes of learning.

The sessions were really interesting professional development. For the senior leaders, we learnt a lot about the content of different subjects and also about the thinking of the subject or phase leader. I was particularly interested in the match between the key components of the planning process contained within the Trust's policy and the extent to which they were realised in practice. On more than one occasion a middle leader would say, 'Oh I understand now, that makes sense' as I explained the inclusion of a particular aspect of the planning process or the connections between various elements. My main takeaways from the numerous discussions were that we had moved a very long way in curriculum planning and yet there was still so much left to do. Key to this was that the initial professional development had been a useful start, but we had failed to recognise the importance and need for on-going professional development to support the middle leaders' improvement of the planning process. Another feedback loop had informed us about what to do next; curriculum development is inexorable but so is the associated professional development.

It is crucial to lock quality into any process, rather than finding out after the event that poor or unthinking implementation has let you down yet again. When utilised in an improvement orientated manner, the three accountability tools – evaluation by design, audit and feedback loops – sit at the heart of a self-improvement culture. This is due to their ability to support improvements during rather than after the event. They promote the systemic use of data, moving it to the heart of the developmental process. The three tools also have the benefit of being used as analytical tools alongside colleagues in a 'do with' rather than 'do to' approach to leadership. This enables a 'no blame, find out and fix it' approach to improvement.

Accountability and professional development are closely related, particularly where the accountability focus is on evaluation, assuring quality, and responsive leadership. In fact, where an organisation has a balanced, intelligent accountability system, I would suggest that accountability may be more correctly viewed as organisational learning. The organisation has put in place processes to educate itself. Further, the evaluation processes, audit outcomes and feedback loops invariably identify training or professional development needs. It is why the Basics of Guardianship and the Expertise are closely associated in this book, as they are in reality. They are both important Ways of Doing.

Basic 8: Expertise

The importance of developing people within the organisation

An effective leader educates, trains and empowers people to realise their full potential. This maximises the capacity within the organisation to maintain high performance and for improvement. They enable a mastery culture, focused on building curriculum, teaching, learning and leadership expertise.

Summary

- The pursuit of mastery is at the heart of developing expertise. Leaders must accept responsibility for building a mastery culture and the norms to support it.
- Leaders must ensure the content, processes and systems relating to professional development create an inevitability that all staff will approach mastery. The same is true for leadership development.
- Expertise is part of a positive synergistic process that both builds and enables the establishment of a high trust culture.
- Autonomy should increase in direct proportion to expertise. Professional support should be greatest where expertise is yet to be developed.
- Auditing and reviewing professional development, with the assistance of external experts, provides an effective means for continuous improvement of the systems and processes in place.
- Too much professional development is viewed from the perspective of provision rather than impact. Evaluating the impact of professional development is a blind spot across much of the school system.
- Orientating professional development towards consideration of impact seeks to consider evidence of the impact of teaching on the quantum of learning. It creates a link between the curriculum and professional development.
- Invariably, one of the greatest blocks to professional development is the lack of time. Leaders need to systematically ensure time is available for people to undertake appropriate professional development. Once time has been created, the content or focus and quality of professional development may be addressed.
- Performance management systems too often have the feeling of being 'done to' rather than 'done with' people. Linking performance reviews to pay and the setting of statistically dubious targets for individual teachers damages a potentially useful developmental process.
- Using the curriculum as the progression model helps teachers more clearly and accurately articulate which aspects of their current teaching practices could be considered a strength and which areas need development. This creates bitesize, actionable professional development opportunities.
- A key question in any professional development system is, 'What was the impact on pupils' outcomes of the professional development you undertook last year?'
- Improving the curriculum requires high quality professional development to be an integral part of the improvement process. If teachers are not to become dis-spirited, curriculum development must be a gradual cumulative process in which teachers are personally involved.
- Leaders need to choose wisely and strategically the most appropriate organisations to work in partnership with, to help elevate their current practice.

Expertise

Educators just cannot help themselves. Each engagement is an opportunity to learn and grow the performance of self, others, the organisation and ultimately the system. These engagements need to be co-ordinated through systems, processes and practices orientated towards mastery; the desire to get better and better at something that matters. Mastery is a long-term commitment that abides by three laws. It is a mindset, a pain, and an asymptote (Pink, 2009):

- Mastery is something a person believes can be developed by working hard at the right things.
- It is this effort, over an extended period, which requires significant commitment particularly when the going gets tough.
- True mastery is always just beyond our reach.

The pursuit of mastery is at the heart of developing the Basic of Expertise. It is the cumulative effect of praxis, an iterative process of thought and action. Leaders must accept responsibility for building a mastery culture and the norms to support it. This includes removing barriers to the development of expertise and determining what will further elevate current practice.

Two problems often encountered by those on the receiving end of professional development are that it is not very good, and it is not very useful. If leaders want people to embrace rather than endure the professional development on offer it must be of high quality and impactful. The development of expertise cannot be accidental or become the domain of a few interested or highly motivated staff. Leaders must ensure the content, processes, and systems relating to professional development create an inevitability that all staff approach mastery in terms of their classroom practice. The same must be applied to leadership development.

The Basic of Expertise is part of a positive synergistic process that both builds and enables the establishment of a high trust culture. This is one in which people feel safe to share significant weaknesses in their practice in order to elicit support. With increasing expertise people must be granted greater professional autonomy, and autonomy should increase in direct proportion to expertise. Professional support should be greatest where expertise is yet to be developed. Building such a culture requires a highly competent organisational approach to the professional development of staff, and achieving this is likely to require support from external experts. To help us, we became part of the Teacher Development Trust (TDT) network.

CPD peer reviews (TDT)

The Teacher Development Trust (TDT) is an independent charity, brilliantly led by David Weston, 'dedicated to improving the educational outcomes of children by ensuring they experience the most effective learning'. The charity's focus is on enhancing teachers' practice through the effective use of professional development. Two standout aspects of their work are their CPD peer reviews and a project report on *Developing Great Teaching* written by a team led by Professor Philippa Cordingley (2015).

The first of our three CPD peer reviews was conducted in November 2013 by Bridget Clay from the TDT and Dave Jones, who would become headteacher of Meols Cop High School, Southport. The process involved completing a self-audit tool (levels were bronze, silver and gold), a series of online staff questionnaires, and a day spent with various groups of staff discussing their experience of professional development. From completing the self-audit tool, I could see that we were on the proverbial journey, and in certain areas we were taking no more than the first few tentative steps.

The CPD peer review looked across a range of related areas: leadership and culture; learning and pedagogy; evaluation of impact; support and challenge; processes, systems and resourcing; and research, innovation and evidence. Completing the Evaluation of Impact section was a sobering experience, and it soon became obvious that this was a real weakness in our practice. I would go as far as saying it was actually a blind spot for me and the school, as it still is across much of the school system. Inevitably, this was highlighted in the final report as a suggested area for development, 'There could be more rigour including a pre- and post- test around CPD processes, and teachers could be engaged further in measuring and evaluating the impact of their CPD.' Additional suggestions were: checking how evidence-based external providers were, and encouragement to engage in more large scale research projects. Despite various attempts to become involved in larger scale research we always seemed to end up in the control group. While an important part of any study it felt a bit second best. The other areas we addressed systematically.

It is important when considering reports of the type produced during the TDT CPD audit, that leaders do not fall into the trap of wondering whether they are fair or not. It is wrong thinking and people can too easily become defensive, which often leads to the opportunity to learn being lost. No report will ever be totally accurate, they are snapshots in time based on the evidence available and the best judgements of the people involved, and as such can be very useful. While not rejecting difficult messages just because they make tough reading, leaders need to apply their own knowledge alongside the fresh insights.

The use of the term 'suggested', with respect to the areas for development, encapsulated the professional way in which the review was conducted. The limitations of the process and levels of certainty that could be ascribed to any conclusions reached had been clearly considered. While the process was very thorough and rigorous, there was a gentleness to the conclusions reached that invited you to consider the way forward. It felt non-threatening and aimed at helping the school to improve the quality and impact of the professional development offered. The bronze level awarded was reflective of where we were at that point in time, and while judgements had been made, the process did not feel judgemental.

Particularly encouraging was a recognition within the audit that 'Regular discussions around teaching and learning and pedagogy take place both formally (in meetings) and informally (for example in staffroom discussions)'. This was considered to be at the gold level. It was supported by the comment, 'The (staff) survey suggests a vast number of informal conversations around teaching and learning, although only half of respondents discuss the best way to teach things in half of departmental meetings or more'. While there was clearly a need to ensure consistently good use of all departmental meetings to discuss planning, pedagogy and assessment, it provided a strong basis on which to move forward.

It is interesting to reflect on why there was a 'vast amount' of discussion around teaching, learning and pedagogy and how leaders influence this. The 2013 CPD peer review was conducted as the school was coming to the end of the massive capital building programme. As part of this process, I had written and shared a series of papers with staff about the school's mission and ethos, as the new buildings needed to be filled with a renewed sense of purpose. Alongside the mission and ethos papers, I had also written and shared a series of six papers based on *Visible Learning* (Hattie, 2009). *Visible Learning* was my entry into a different way of thinking about school improvement, it was a movement away from the anecdotal towards more evidence-informed decisions. As leaders we must reinforce the behaviours we want to see in others by modelling them ourselves. People take note of what you say, particularly when it accords with what you do. John Hattie's work led me into the twin worlds of 'what works' and 'what matters'. This significantly influenced my conversations and actions during my final decade in school leadership.

181

Also coming out as a strength in the CPD report was the provision of time for people to undertake appropriate professional development. Invariably, one of the greatest blocks to professional development is the lack of time in people's busy working and home lives. Once time has been created, the challenge moves to the content or focus, and quality of professional development. This needs to be systematically addressed. We had a long-established shorter teaching day each week which increased the opportunity for professional development from 3:00pm to 5:00pm. The number of Inset days taken each year was increased to seven, with nine taken in 2015/16 when curriculum changes were at a peak in primary and secondary schools.

Alongside this we had created the opportunity for groups of staff to take forward an area of professional interest with associated resourcing. More often than not these initiatives required time for collaborative planning, peer observation or visiting another school. These were resourced with 'cover vouchers' that could be used to free staff for the time required. This idea later morphed into a reduction in teaching time of approximately an hour a week for all staff, in return for a commitment to enhanced personal professional development. This commitment, alongside a greater focus on the impact of professional development, was captured in a totally revamped performance management and appraisal system.

Rethinking performance management

Performance management systems too often have the feeling of being 'done to' rather than 'done with' people. Linking these performance reviews to pay caused damage to the process as did the setting of statistically dubious targets for individual teachers. The almost universal and unhelpful use of graded lesson observations was a part of performance management. This high stakes system was something to be endured rather than effectively utilised to develop greater expertise. Having been completed, many reviews were destined to gather dust on a shelf rather than being an integral part of a system to help staff develop and improve their performance. As a school, we were guilty of all these errors.

Following a decision to change our processes, the first thing we did was to uncouple the link between performance management and annual pay reviews. In short, we got rid of annual performance pay and moved back to automatic pay progression. Taking pay off the table created a lower stakes system that allowed a greater focus on professional development. Another enabler was to produce a core set of three objectives for all teaching staff.

The first core objective focused on the 'Quality of teaching, assessment and learning leading to high standards and progress particularly for the most disadvantaged pupils'. The other two focused on contributing to the Catholic ethos of the school and professional development. We set three standards for each of the objectives: Qualified Teacher (M1-3), Experienced Teacher (M4-6), and Expert Teacher (UPR1-3). One of the aspects which changed as a teacher moved from the standards set for qualified to expert, was the expectation that more experienced and expert teachers would seek to impact positively beyond their own classroom, at a departmental or phase or whole school level. That is, with experience comes the responsibility to support and develop colleagues. It is a Silicon Valley way of working with an expectation of collaborative practice and the sharing of knowledge, which is explored further in the next chapter. The use of an agreed set of core objectives allowed time for a more introspective analysis and then discussion of the individual's practice, impact, and future development needs.

The new performance management and appraisal system consisted of a series of discussion prompts. In the one below, for pupil progress, you can see the influence of Professor John Hattie's work:

- Looking at the evidence from across last year's classes/subjects; in what aspects was there one year or more progress for one year's teaching? In which aspects was this not so?

It is a really interesting question that asks a teacher to think about what constitutes a year's progress and how it might be assessed. By this point we had already moved to the curriculum as the progression model with assessments seeking to identify what pupils did and did not know, and could and could not do. It helped teachers more clearly and accurately articulate which aspects of their current teaching practices could be considered a strength and which areas needed development. It is this more detailed analysis – moving away from considering ourselves as outstanding, good, requires improvement or inadequate teachers – that creates bitesize, actionable professional development opportunities.

The next set of prompts focused on the professional development that was at the heart of the new system. The first point for discussion I would have struggled to answer throughout my career:

- What was the impact on pupils' outcomes of the professional development you undertook last year?

For all the professional development I undertook, I can honestly say I had never sought to assess it from the perspective of impact on pupil outcomes. In many ways this question was one of the key takeaways from the first TDT

CPD peer audit. For far too long I had been viewing professional development from a provision perspective – what was being offered – rather than an impact one. Orientating professional development towards consideration of impact gives a very different perspective to a teacher. It also creates a very different way of thinking and working. It takes the profession away from a descriptive anecdotal paradigm that tends to determine the quality of teaching on the basis of what a person does, towards a more evaluative one. The evaluation seeks to consider evidence of the impact of teaching on the quantum of learning. This may be extrapolated backwards to the professional development undertaken or forwards to what is required. It creates a link between curriculum and professional development.

> *Attempts to produce 'teacher-free' material have foundered simply because in any classroom the influence of the teacher exceeds that of any materials. One cannot impose a curriculum on a teacher ... Once this is accepted, the logical consequence is that curriculum development must start from the teacher. Teachers must be helped to overcome weaknesses and exploit their strengths ...*
>
> (Howson, 1979)

Improving the curriculum requires high quality professional development to be an integral part of the improvement process. If teachers are not to become dis-spirited, curriculum development must be a gradual cumulative process in which teachers are personally involved. There are numerous ways in which teachers can provide peer subject or phase support on important areas such as helping others improve their content knowledge and pedagogical knowledge.

The next question in the process, with its set of prompts, read, 'What area of professional development would most help and support your further development as a teacher this year?'

- Subject and subject pedagogical knowledge
- Curriculum, assessment and examination or qualification changes
- General pedagogy and understanding how pupils learn
- Developing the Catholic ethos
- Other

While the question appears fairly benign, a sting came in the follow-up to it, 'What evidence have you used to identify this aspect of professional practice?' It was an attempt to address what Howson (1979) proposed, namely, 'Teachers must be helped to overcome weaknesses and exploit their strengths'. This is the first step in actually identifying them accurately.

Older teachers may remember a time when the local authority CPD course folder would land in September, and you would have a quick look to see if there was anything you fancied; and if there was you could duly sign up with the school's permission. Moving to an evaluation of practice as the first step in the process of determining the most appropriate professional development to engage in creates the need for teachers to look at evidence of its impact. Many of our teachers used their analyses of pupils' assessments to identify what they had or had not taught well as the basis for discussion. This is why reforming performance management requires it to be dissociated from pay progression. It is unreasonable to expect teachers to expose their vulnerability by being honest and open about their professional weaknesses, particularly if it means their pay may be adversely affected. This is where leaders need wisdom to align whole systems with the desirable outcomes sought.

The final parts of the performance management involved discussions about the enhanced professional development that would be undertaken during the year and wider career aspirations, alongside the professional development that may help support them. This revised approach to performance management and professional development evolved over a couple of years involving discussions with staff, unions and directors. It incorporated emerging evidence of what constituted the most effective practice. The whole aim was to align performance management within the Basic of Expertise.

Developing great teaching

The *Developing Great Teaching* report (Cordingley, 2015) identified eight key elements of professional development. The elements were: the duration and rhythm of effective support; the consideration of participants' needs; alignment of professional development processes, content, and activities; the content of effective professional development; activities associated with effective professional development; the role of external providers and specialists; collaboration and peer learning; and leadership around professional development. Taking the report and reading it with senior leaders across the Trust, we could see areas where we were aligned with the recommendations, and places where we were not.

One of the phrases that hit me quite powerfully was concerned with the duration of professional development; 'to transform general practice, longer duration seems key' (Cordingley, 2015). The suggestion was that a professional development programme of 'at least two terms – more usually a year (or longer)' was required to produce 'profound, lasting change' in a teacher's classroom practice.

Too often a single Inset day or after school session is expected to substantially change or enhance teachers' practice. In some schools, teaching school alliances, and local authorities there is a conveyor belt of weekly or fortnightly discrete sessions that teachers endure. There is no time available for them to embrace a potential pedagogical change before the next session is upon them. In moving away from a 'content blunderbuss' approach towards professional development programmes that extended for the full academic year, we were able to also address issues relating to effective support (rhythm) and consider the needs of different participants. The leadership of professional development was enhanced by these changes. The vision for professional learning had greater clarity, professional development was better organised and resourced, and more people became involved in delivering professional development.

By the time of the next TDT CPD Audit in 2016, a number of the changes we had made were beginning to bear fruit and the bronze award became silver. In 2019, the school achieved a TDT gold award with the particular strengths identified as a very strong and open culture, evidence woven into many school processes and staff thinking deeply and critically about it (due in no small part to the influence of the research school), and again an acknowledgement of the very generous allocation of time and resources for CPD.

The gold level report contained suggestions about whether performance management could be strengthened through more regular check-ins particularly around the use of enhanced professional development time, reintroducing lesson observations in a diagnostic or formative format, and strengthening the links between our work on curriculum planning, CPD, disciplined inquiry and the school's approach to the analysis of pupil assessments. These were all useful suggestions that could help further hone the professional development available to staff.

Improvement is inexorable and often best carried out in partnership with others. The Teacher Development Trust was one of a number of organisations that helped elevate our practice.

Choosing the right elevators

All organisations have capacity for improvement and maintaining high standards, and part of the challenge of leadership is to further develop this capacity. The most effective leaders intentionally build the professional development and training systems and processes that enable staff, as well as pupils, to flourish. This often involves using the expertise of others to help elevate practice.

Appearing on one of the opening pages of *Liminal Leadership* is the following: 'External forces and pressures may restrict you but they do not define you. You are defined by your 'why' and the integrity with which you pursue it.' It is also true that external forces and opportunities may help enhance your work. Engagement with the Teacher Development Trust is one such example, becoming a research school was another. Both of these were intentional, we deliberately chose to become part of these networks. They were external opportunities that helped enhance the quality of professional development offered to staff, and they became key elevators in moving St. Mary's and the Trust forward. In time, we would also make use of the Apprenticeship Levy as another key elevator.

The Apprenticeship Levy

One of the suggestions made in the TDT 2019 report related to support staff, in particular those who were classroom-based. This group of staff were less positive about the development opportunities available to them, and although other groups of support staff were not mentioned I think such feelings might have been equally applicable to them. The Apprenticeship Levy, introduced in April 2017, provided a resource that we could use to elevate our practice.

The Apprenticeship Levy is an 'all age' fund that can be used to meet the costs associated with the training and assessment elements of an apprenticeship for new and existing staff. It was first brought to my attention by our finance manager who had been tracking the funds we had been paying into the Levy. We initially used it to fund Level 2 training for all our cleaners. Two things about the impact of this training are noteworthy.

First, we found that the turnover of cleaners significantly reduced. Due to Blackpool's tourism industry there was a tendency for some cleaners to seek jobs in schools during the winter, only to leave in the spring when more hours of work became available in hotels, even when the hourly pay was lower. Providing this training emphasised the importance of the cleaners to our organisation. As the old story goes, when a visitor to NASA asked a cleaner what she did, her reply was 'I put people on the moon'. It reminds us of the collective importance and contribution of all staff to an organisation's mission. Our cleaners were part of the team that helped educate children and young people. Secondly the quality of cleaning improved as staff used correct processes for cleaning rooms and specialist areas like toilets. One of the things I found out was that pupil toilets should be cleaned using three different coloured cloths. The different colours are so germs are not transferred between basins and toilets. One cloth is used for basins and two further different coloured cloths are required for the toilets. You should never the same cloth for the inside and outside of the toilet! The training ensured people knew what to do.

As well as existing staff, we used the levy to train new staff when the school employed a trainee ICT technician, a receptionist and a clerk in the finance office. Despite our spending, the funds continued to build up in the Apprenticeship Levy. We then started to use the Levy to fund a series of programmes for teachers, including a combined Senior Leaders Masters/Level 7 programme with the National College of Education, which is a programme I now tutor on.

Despite the real benefits the Apprenticeship Levy can bring an organisation, it is significantly under-utilised. The Levy is a use it or lose it fund. If the funding, which is contributed on a monthly basis, is not used within 24 months it is reclaimed by HMRC. The amount of Apprenticeship Levy funding being returned is genuinely shocking. Through a Freedom of Information request to three local authorities, I found out that from April 2017 to early 2021 the local authorities had received £9,453,840 of funds into their accounts from community and voluntary controlled schools. In the same time period the local authorities only spent £2,145,286 on apprenticeship programmes for staff employed by the schools while returning £3,569,857 of unused Apprenticeship Levy to HMRC.

It is important to note that some of the returned funds are likely to have come from other departments within the local authorities, but the wasted opportunities are significant. There may well be similar issues in multi-academy trusts – who hold the Levy for their academies – but the scale is likely to be smaller as most have fewer schools. The Apprenticeship Levy provides a real opportunity to invest in all staff. It was and continues to be a key elevator. So too was our work as a research school.

Research Schools Network

The Education Endowment Foundation (EFF) and the Institute for Effective Education (IEE) collaborated to form a network of schools that would support evidence-based practice. Naming them research schools caused some confusion initially. Their role was not to undertake research, rather it was to 'share what they know about putting research into practice, and support schools in their region to make better use of evidence to inform their teaching and learning'. Each designated research school was involved in three key strands of work: engaging other schools with the evidence and evidence-based practice; supporting teachers and schools to use evidence-based practice; and disciplined innovation, evaluation and encouraging participation in wider research.

To enable these three key strands of work there was a requirement to build internal capacity. This involved establishing a team to work on research school programmes and developing the organisation's understanding and use of evidence-based practice. These provided strong foundations on which to develop relationships with a network of local schools and in turn influence their use of evidence and evidence-based practice.

Our first application to become a research school, submitted in December 2016, received a 'highly commended'. In short, we were unsuccessful but received positive and useful feedback. It was suggested that it would be worth our while submitting further applications in other rounds. At about the same time a series of Opportunity Areas were announced by the Secretary of State for Education, Justine Greening MP. Blackpool was to be one of the Opportunity Areas and each one would have a designated research school. Following a second application and interview, St. Mary's was designated the research school for the Blackpool Opportunity Area from September 2017.

While the timing of the Opportunity Areas was extremely fortuitous to us becoming a research school, the school's designation was not simply down to good luck. Over time, leaders create a sense of direction – identifying key elevators and enablers to support their journey – while also accepting that there may well be an element of serendipity in any successful outcome. The development of staff, and the explicit building of capacity within the organisation had always been central to my leadership philosophy.

Our first attempt to become involved in delivering initial and on-going professional development at a local and regional level started in the Autumn term of 2003 in what was my third year of headship, when we applied to become one of a national network of training schools. Training schools were required to deliver initial teacher training (ITT) and on-going professional development in collaboration with other schools and providers. St. Mary's was already heavily involved in ITT, supporting many trainee teacher placements in various subjects. This was in partnership with two local Higher Education institutions and occasionally ones from further afield. Key to the decision to pursue the training school designation was its link to an existing strength.

We spent time developing the training school bid and the associated network. Following the inevitable last minute pre-deadline rush, we sent our bid in and waited for the response. When the letter eventually landed it informed us that the training school programme was under review, and we never heard anything else. Despite the less than auspicious start we continued to seek opportunities to engage in collaboratively delivering and developing education and training.

Leadership development

Alongside our involvement with ITT we were also taking our first tentative steps in helping develop the next generation of school leaders. In the early phase, this involved working as a placement school for colleagues undertaking their National Professional Qualification for Headship. The two-week placement, often spread over a number of terms, allowed the placement school to share its areas of strength. In return, the visiting senior leader would undertake a leadership project to help develop practice at the school. The projects undertaken by the senior leader were based on their interests and strengths, and our genuine areas for development. Their final reports were presented to the appropriate governing body committee for information and further action. One of the factors that made these placements so valuable was that they were a voluntary part of the development programme. This allowed for a genuine openness from the people involved and interest to learn from and with each other.

Following involvement with the Specialist Schools and Academy Trust's (SSAT) System Redesign Group, I was invited to present at a number of their leadership development programmes. Being asked to present on leadership was interesting and challenging in equal measure, and when putting together presentations you soon expose where your knowledge, thinking or experience lack depth. There can also be a tendency to become overly descriptive, 'We did this ... then this ... then this'. While describing what you did helps people understand a particular approach or project, they are often more interested in why you did it and what you might do differently in the future. This adds extra dimensions to any presentation, and communicates both leadership purpose and learning.

Over time, I became the course leader for one of the SSAT's programmes which in turn led to the school becoming a SSAT leadership hub. It was the school's first real experience of trying to lead at a local and regional level. One important lesson we learnt was the need for sufficient and appropriate capacity to engage externally without damaging the internal operation of the school. This was reinforced in one of the five sections of the research school planning document which was dedicated to building internal capacity. I assumed responsibility for the overall leadership of the research school, and we appointed from internal senior leader applications two research school leads. They jointly shared three days of time committed to research school work. In addition, we already had a team of five CUREE (Centre for the Use of Research and Evidence in Education) trained 'research champions' and two Trust-level assistant headteachers – one with overall responsibility for literacy and the other for mathematics – who added further capacity. We appointed additional administrative staff and directed some of the ICT technician team's time towards research school work. This group of people formed the initial research school team.

The national research school team challenged us to go further with respect to two aspects of planning. One was to consider succession planning as part of the longer term sustainability of our work as a research school. The other related to building a greater degree of understanding across our own organisation about the use of evidence and evidence-based practice, and it was this which proved to be by far the greater challenge. As a profession, we are still in the infancy of developing this understanding with a wide range of approaches from early adopters to laggards. The use of research findings in education is challenging for a number of reasons.

Professor Christian Bokhove (2018) provides five useful pieces of advice for those engaging with education research. While education research is important it is also messy. The soft knowledge associated with education research – due to the unpredictability of humans and the impact of teachers' values and beliefs on the matters being researched – makes it difficult to be definitive about cause and effect. The incremental nature of research means that the cumulative gains in knowledge, added through each successive study, lead towards a scientific consensus that is organic in nature. This is difficult for the teacher or school leader who needs to act now and wants to know which approach is best. It is exacerbated by concerns over the impact of context on implementation and the extent to which metrics – what we choose to measure, how we measure it and whether we measure what we value – add to the complexity of understanding and determining how best to use the evidence available.

Route 128 and Silicon Valley
Working as a research school and as part of an Opportunity Area needed to be co-ordinated at a strategic level. It is where the enhanced leadership knowledge across a range of domains, the specialist domain knowledge of education, and an understanding of the local context needed to be brought together. It is too

easy to fall into the leadership trap of seeing and behaving as if the different partnerships, with their associated funding, are discrete; what I would term a silo approach. Leaders are required to create a synergy between the distinct parts so that the implementation feels to be one holistic programme. I wrote about this in more detail in Chapter 12.

At the core of the literacy programme were the twin elements of improving Key Stage 3 literacy and developing a more evidence-informed approach to school improvement. Funding from the Opportunity Area and Right to Succeed helped develop capacity and a more evidence-based approach across Blackpool secondary schools. The latter was a key objective for the research school that in turn provided much of the training and development to support the Key Stage 3 literacy programme leaders. These two different strands of work were brought together in a synergistic manner.

From my earliest days as a leader, the development of self and others has always been a fascination and a high priority. Leading, working alongside others, and engaging in various professional development opportunities, I consider as the most important uses of my time. For leaders the balance between their responsibilities to develop people who will improve their own organisation, and accepting that a number will move on, can be a challenge. In a disgruntled moment early in headship, I took myself down a cul-de-sac of thought; if striving to develop our staff meant we 'lost' some of them, then maybe we would be better off not making them so capable. It reminded me of the story of Route 128 and Silicon Valley.

Professor David Hargreaves (2012) tells the story of the world renowned high-tech innovation hub in San Francisco and the much less well known Route 128, near Boston. The variation in success between the two high-tech centres is due to the difference placed on competition and co-operation by the firms making them up. It is a lesson that the education system would do well to learn. The companies that made up Route 128 had centralised decision making hierarchies with a vertical flow of information and close guarding of corporate knowledge. Employees were expected to remain loyal to the company. This produced a competitive system based upon independent companies. In contrast, companies in Silicon Valley, while still competing with one another, put in place opportunities for collaborative practice – dense social networks and open labour markets – and the sharing of knowledge between teams in different companies. The success of Silicon Valley was built upon high levels of social capital and its two constituent elements: trust and reciprocity. It is these high levels of trust and reciprocity that the school system will need to build if high standards of teaching and leadership practice are to be distributed fully across the system.

When Teaching School Alliances started to develop after 2010, we became involved as strategic partners in two alliances. Teaching Schools had six main priorities – often referred to as the 'Big 6': initial teacher training (ITT); continuing professional development (CPD) and leadership development; specialist leaders in education (SLEs); school to school support; succession planning; and research and development. I have always had some mixed feelings about the whole Teaching School programme.

The involvement of schools in leading on teacher training and development, and supporting other schools are both commendable. Positive aspects of greater school involvement in ITT were seen in some alliances, with the school-based experience of trainees significantly enhanced with improved programmes, oversight, mentoring and engagement with current teachers. However, this was not universally true and the variability between programmes and Teaching Schools meant some trainees failed to get the best possible start to their careers.

Engagement in ITT enables organisations to increase teacher numbers across the system and help with their own recruitment of new staff. The balance of these two points is crucial. The primary driver for supporting ITT must be system-serving not self-serving. Sadly, this is not always the case, and there are too many stories of current Teaching Schools creaming off the best trainee teachers into their schools for it not to be a concern. With Ofsted 'outstanding' being a pre-requisite for designation as a Teaching School, and with 'outstanding' schools quite substantially and disproportionately identified in the most affluent areas of the country, there is a real danger of the 'Matthew effect'. Schools serving the most disadvantaged communities have last call on the available teaching pool. This is where clarity around moral purpose is so important in leadership.

With respect to the CPD and leadership development strand, I was actively involved with delivery of the National Professional Qualifications (NPQs). While thoroughly enjoying working with other senior leaders – tutors and participants – I cannot help but feel that the NPQs were rather stilted. CPD flourished in terms of provision, but there seemed little evidence of evaluation to determine impact. At its worst some Teaching School CPD calendars became a series of one or two session taster events that had little depth and even less chance of having a significant impact on teachers' practice.

Many teachers benefitted from designation as Specialist Leaders of Education but far fewer actually engaged in school-to-school improvement work. Anecdotally, where there was engagement often both the SLE and the people who worked with them appreciated the opportunity. At its best, open, professional, mutually beneficial relationships were established between the two parties. Where things were less successful SLEs from 'outstanding' schools struggled to understand the complexity and context of working in a school with large numbers of disadvantaged pupils. Staff working in schools with large numbers of disadvantaged pupils might well have been less than enamoured by another imposed, even if well-meaning, intervention being done to them rather than with them.

The education system seems caught between Route 128 and Silicon Valley. There have been attempts by various governments over the past few decades to build a Silicon Valley approach to the training and on-going professional development of staff. It has unfortunately morphed into a more Route 128 approach with an increase in central control and micromanagement of schools. Ideology is presented as evidence and politics replaces partnerships. For example, the enemies of promise and the blob rhetoric – anti local authority and Higher Education – sees political preference driving policy. This is not a great starting point for building the trust and reciprocity required to engage and empower the full system.

We cannot have a system where anything goes, and all is of equal value. This allows for some poor practice at best, and some absolute rubbish at worst, to be foisted on children and young people. However, neither can we permit a system in which there is only one right way imposed on schools. Rather there is a wisdom place that empowers a well-educated profession to align beliefs about the purpose of education and the values that should be at its heart, the content that should be taught to and the empowerment of the next generation, evidence about how this may best be done, and high quality enabling implementation informed by experience, to all come together to help lever school and system wide improvements. This requires high quality enabling leadership, the practical wisdom embodied in phronesis, built upon the Ways of Being, Ways of Knowing and Ways of Doing.

Getting back to the basics

Three frogs sat on a lily pad. Two of them thought about jumping off.
How many frogs are left on the lily pad?

The answer is three. Two of them only thought about jumping off.
They did not actually do it.

The three wise frogs: Being, Knowing and Doing

While thinking and acting are distinct entities, in leadership they work best in an iterative process. This praxis allied to a virtuous approach which seeks to do what is good and right, creates a leadership trivium. The three ways – Being, Knowing and Doing – and their constituent Basics are mutually supportive and synergistic in nature.

A balanced view of leadership places an equal priority on the eight Basics. These sit at the core of effective leadership and it is important to have a level of competency in each. The Basics of Purpose and Introspection, Specialism and Strategy and Implementation, Networking, Guardianship and Expertise, are entwined strands. The whole is greater than the sum of the parts. While this may initially feel overwhelming, each of us will be able to look at the eight

Basics and identify ones that are relative strengths and others that we need to work at. This is the start of a process that enables us to intentionally grow and improve as leaders. A combination of increased knowledge, practice and experience, and reflection, will over time allow us to improve those areas where we are weak or simply have no knowledge or experience.

I have always maintained my fascination with aspects of curriculum design, how content is structured, pedagogy, assessment and the optimum conditions for learning. Being given opportunities to lead from an early stage in my career, I learnt how to turn ideas into the lived experiences of teachers and young people. As my career advanced, I had to move beyond my own resources as a leader and consider who or what might be able to elevate our practice. The accountability system was never far away. Going back to the Basics of Purpose while also learning from the writings, presentation and working of others, I started to develop a more sophisticated and counter-cultural understanding of how accountability may support school improvement. Over the years, it taught me too many bad habits and too much bad practice. It was towards the latter part of my career I started to understand accountability from the wider perspective of guardianship.

However, much of the detailed strategic knowledge I now possess, I developed once in headship. Prior to this I had some limited knowledge of how finance worked at a whole school level but knew absolutely nothing about premises development. During my time as a school leader I was responsible for oversight of capital programmes totalling well over £30 million. It is the combination of a willingness to learn, identification and targeting of the key professional areas for improvement, and effective professional development that help form the most capable leaders. Without these there are implications for leadership in the absence of one or more of the Ways or one of their constituent Basics.

In the absence of Being the organisation may well lack purpose. Leaders' behaviours may become dubious or at times unethical. Without the necessary introspection both personal and organisational growth are less likely. There is a real risk the organisation and its leaders will become aimless, self-serving and stuck. The aimless organisation, without a clear sense of purpose, can be easily spotted. It becomes inward looking, excuses-orientated and slow to improve. Alternatively, with no underlying narrative to guide it, it adopts every new idea only to jettison it before moving rapidly to the latest next best thing. These are Fullan's (2000) 'Christmas tree schools'; all show and busyness but with little real substance. The organisation has lost the capacity to discern what is important and what is peripheral. The leadership mentality is defensive and there is no thought given to engagement with the wider system at a personal or organisational level.

In the absence of Knowing, thought and consequentially actions are based on ignorance. There is a lack of knowledge to effectively guide thinking, discussions and decision making. This will inevitably lead to poor decisions about development and improvement priorities. It will also severely affect strategic decision making. Financial, legal, staffing, safeguarding or health and safety may all potentially come under strain. This does not simply limit the development of the organisation, it can all too often put school leaders in legal difficulties and conflict with governors, the local community or unions and professional associations. It may also lead to the unfocused busyness associated with unnecessary and unproductive workload.

In the absence of Doing, a combination of poor implementation, a lack of positive relationships, low standards not being addressed and a lack of professional development can lead to organisational inertia. The outcome is well-meaning and knowledgeable leaders essentially going nowhere. Alternatively, there may be a lot of activity but not much movement. In time, external changes will leave the organisation exposed.

It does not have to be that way. What is required is an investment in the formation of leaders that is substantial and significant. This investment must support leaders into the role and continue when they are in post, creating a positive cumulative impact. The development of leaders must be broad yet focused; it needs to look at leadership from the perspective of alignment rather than the creation of dichotomies.

There is a need to contextualise purpose using specialist domain knowledge that engages with strategy to ensure high quality implementation. The building of capacity and capabilities through the professional development of people to support implementation, with external expertise as required. This sits alongside evaluative processes, the use of periodic audit checks and effective feedback loops to ensure leaders know how things are going and where to go next. The more personal introspective, reflective feedback loops help leaders in their own development.

My hope and intention, in writing *Leadership: Being, Knowing, Doing*, was to help leaders. Leadership can be learnt. The three Ways with their constituent Basics are a means of exploring leadership. They represent a window or a mirror to help leaders improve their practice. In turn, as leaders, we must support the leaders who follow, who we have a responsibility to intentionally and collectively form.

References

Allen, R. (2019) Careering towards a curriculum crash? *Musings on education policy.* https://rebeccaallen.co.uk/2019/12/04/careering-towards-a-curriculum-crash/

Allen-Kinross, P. (2019) Schools with deprived pupils 'still less likely to be judged good', admits Ofsted. *Schoolsweek,* October 29. https://schoolsweek.co.uk/schools-with-deprived-pupils-still-less-likely-to-be-judged-good-admits-ofsted/

ASCL (2019) *Framework for ethical leadership in education.* ASCL Professional Development Online. https://www.ascl.org.uk/Help-and-Advice/Leadership-and-governance/Strategic-planning/Framework-for-ethical-leadership-in-education

Bauersfeld, H. (1979) Research related to the mathematical learning process. In International Commission on Mathematical Instruction (ed.), *New trends in mathematical teaching* (Vol. IV, pp. 199-213). Paris, France: UNESCO.

Bergman, P. (2018) Execution is a people problem, not a strategy problem. In *The chief strategy officer playbook: How to transform strategies into great results.* Wargrave: Thinkers50 Ltd.

Biggs, J. B. and Collis, K. F. (1982) *Evaluating the quality of learning: The SOLO Taxonomy (structure of the observed learning outcome).* New York: Academic Press.

Bokhove, C. (2018) 5 Things you need to know about research. *TES blog.* https://www.tes.com/magazine/article/5-things-you-need-know-about-research

Brennan, G. (2013) How can schools prepare for the future? *The Guardian,* June 25. https://www.theguardian.com/teacher-network/2013/jun/25/schools-prepare-for-future-events-tim-brighouse

Bungay, S. (2019) 5 Myths About Strategy. *Harvard Business Review*, April 19. https://hbr.org/2019/04/5-myths-about-strategy

Coe, R. (2014) 'Classroom observation: it's harder than you think'. *Centre for Evaluation and Monitoring blog.* https://www.cem.org/blog/414

Coe, R., Rauch, C. J., Kime, S. and Singleton, D. (2020) *Great Teaching Toolkit: Evidence Review.* Evidence Based Education. https://assets. website-files.com/5ee28729f7b4a5fa99bef2b3/5ee9f507021911ae35a c6c4d_EBE_GTT_EVIDENCE%20REVIEW_DIGITAL.pdf?utm_ referrer=https%3A%2F%2Fwww.greatteaching.com%2F

Cordingley, P., Higgins, S., Greany, T., Buckler, N., Coles-Jordan, D., Crisp, B., Saunders, L. and Coe, R. (2015) *Developing great teaching: lessons from the international reviews into effective professional development.* Project Report. London: Teacher Development Trust.

Covey, S. R. (2004) *The 7 Habits of Highly Effective People: Powerful Lessons in Personal Change. 25th anniversary edition.* New York: Simon and Schuster.

Eacott, S. (2008) Strategy in educational leadership: in search of unity. *Journal of Educational Administration,* (46)3, 353-375.

Education Endowment Foundation (2019) *Putting Evidence to Work – A School's Guide to Implementation.* https://educationendowmentfoundation.org.uk/tools/ guidance-reports/a-schools-guide-to-implementation/

Freire, P. (2017) *Pedagogy of the Oppressed.* London: Penguin.

Fullan, M. (2000). *The Role of the Principal in School Reform.* Occasional Paper Series, 2000 (6). Retrieved from https://educate.bankstreet.edu/occasional-paper-series/vol2000/iss6/2

Gibbons, A. (2021) Food parcels were put ahead of education, says Spielman. *TES,* 14 September. https://www.tes.com/news/food-parcels-were-put-ahead-education-says-spielman

Goleman, D., Boyatzis, R. and McKee, A. (2002) *Primal Leadership.* Boston: Harvard Business School Press.

Hamel, G. and Prahalad, C. K. (1989) *Strategic Intent*. Harvard Business School Press.

Hattie, J. (2009) *Visible Learning: a synthesis of over 800 meta-analyses relating to achievement*. Abingdon: Routledge

Hargreaves, D. H. (2012) *A self-improving school system: towards maturity*. Nottingham: National College for School Leadership.

Hawes, J. (2020) *The Shortest History of England*. Exeter: Old Street Publishing.

Hay Group (2007) *Rush to the Top – Accelerating the Development of Leaders in Schools*. London: Hay Group.

Headteachers Roundtable (2016) The Alternative Green Paper: Schools that enable all to thrive and flourish. *Headteachers Roundtable blog*. https://headteachersroundtable.wordpress.com/alternative-green-paper-2016/

Heath, C. and Heath, D. (2010) *Switch: How to Change Things when Change is Hard*. London: Random House Business Books.

Heath, D. (2020) *Upstream: How to Solve Problems Before They Happen*. London: Bantam Press,

Hill, A., Mellon, L., Laker, B. and Goddard, J. (2016) The One Type of Leader Who Can Turn Around a Failing School. *Harvard Business Review*, October 20. https://hbr.org/2016/10/the-one-type-of-leader-who-can-turn-around-a-failing-school

Hirsch Jr, E. D. (1988) *Cultural Literacy*. New York: Vintage Books.

House, E., Glass, G. V., McLean, L. D. and Walker, D. F. (1978) *No Simple Answer: Critique of the 'Follow Through' Evaluation*. Educational Leadership

Howson, A. G. (1979) *A critical analysis of curriculum development in mathematical education*. In International Commission on Mathematical Instruction (ed.), New trends in mathematical teaching (Vol. IV, pp. 134-161). Paris, France, UNESCO.

Jerrim, J., Sims, S. and Allen, R. (2021) *The mental health and wellbeing of teachers in England*. London: Nuffield Foundation. https://johnjerrim.com/papers/

Kerr, J. (2013) *Legacy*. London: Constable and Robinson.

Kingsnorth, S. (2019) Forget Finland. Could Estonia help to reverse our dire results? *Solomon Kingsnorth blog*. https://medium.com/solomonkingsnorth/forget-finland-could-estonia-help-to-reverse-our-dire-sats-and-gcse-results-b56cd746850a

Laker, B., Cobb, D., and Trehan, R. (2021) *Too Proud to Lead*. London: Bloomsbury Business.

Leithwood, K., Harris, A. and Hopkins, D. (2019) Seven strong claims about successful school leadership revisited. *School Leadership and Management*, DOI: 10.1080/13632434.2019.1596077

Lough, C. (2020) Dylan Wiliam: 'Immoral' to teach 'too full' curriculum. *TES*, 28 April. https://www.tes.com/news/dylan-wiliam-immoral-teach-too-full-curriculum

McInerney, L. (2011) *Ladders, Stairways, Sieves: The basis of Almost All Educational Debate*. The Centre for Education & Youth. https://cfey.org/2011/12/ladders-stairways-sieves-the-basis-of-almost-all-educational-debate/

Munby, S. (2019) *Imperfect Leadership*. Carmarthen: Crown House Publishing.

Mills, I., Ridley, M., Laker, B. and Chapman, T. (2017) *The Salesperson's Secret Code: The belief systems that distinguish winners*. London: LID Publishing Ltd.

Nolan, M. (1995) *The 7 principles of public life*. 1995 Committee on Standards in Public Life. https://www.gov.uk/government/publications/the-7-principles-of-public-life/the-7-principles-of-public-life--2

Nye, P. and Thomson, D. (2018) *Who's Left 2018, part one: The main findings*. FFT Education Datalab. https://ffteducationdatalab.org.uk/2018/06/whos-left-2018-part-one-the-main-findings/

Oehmen, J., Velasco, D. and Willumsen, P. (2018) Four types of strategy work: Choosing the right implementation approach. In *The chief strategy officer playbook: How to transform strategies into great results.* Wargrave: Thinkers50 Ltd.

Ofsted (2019) *Education Inspection Framework* https://www.gov.uk/government/publications/education-inspection-framework

Peters, T. J. and Waterman, R. H. (1982). *In search of excellence: lessons from America's best-run companies.* New York: Harper and Row

Pink, D. (2009) *Drive: The surprising truth about what motivates us.* Edinburgh, Canongate Books Ltd.

Rees, T. (2020) A new perspective for school leadership? *Ambition Institute blog.* https://www.ambition.org.uk/blog/2020-new-perspective-school-leadership/

Reeves, M., Levin, S., Fuller, J. and Hassan, F. (2018) Your Change Needs a Strategy. In *The chief strategy officer playbook: How to transform strategies into great results.* Wargrave: Thinkers50 Ltd.

Roberts, J. (2021) Ofsted admits it failed to flag up off-rolling. *TES,* September 9. https://www.tes.com/news/ofsted-admits-it-failed-clearly-flag-off-rolling-schools

Rohr, R. (2020a) *Our Three Intelligences.* Center for Action and Contemplation. https://cac.org/our-three-intelligences-2020-02-17/

Rohr, R. (2020b) *Simply Living the Gospel.* Center for Action and Contemplation. https://cac.org/simply-living-the-gospel-2020-02-02/

Rohr, R. (2020c) *Knowing from the Bottom.* Center for Action and Contemplation. https://cac.org/knowing-from-the-bottom-2020-02-10/

Rohr, R. (2021) *The Three Domes.* Center for Action and Contemplation. https://cac.org/the-three-domes-2021-01-24/

Rose, W. R. and Cray, D. (2010) Public Sector Strategy Formation. *Canadian Public Administration, 53*(4). https://doi.org/10.1111/j.1754-7121.2010.00145.x

Shulman, L. (2004) *The Wisdom of Practice: Essays on teaching, learning, and learning to teach.* University of Michigan: Jossey-Bass.

Sinek, S. (2009) *Start with Why: How Great Leaders Inspire Everyone to Take Action.* London: Penguin Books Ltd.

Sherrington, T. (2019) *Rosenshine's Principles in Action.* Woodbridge: John Catt Educational Ltd.

Sweller, J., van Merriënboer, J. and Paas, F. (2019). Cognitive Architecture and Instructional Design: 20 Years Later. *Educational Psychology Review, 31*(2), 261-292. https://doi.org/10.1007/s10648-019-09465-5

Thomson, D. (2021) *How much pupil premium funding have schools missed out on.* FFT Education Datalab. https://ffteducationdatalab.org.uk/2021/07/how-much-pupil-premium-funding-have-schools-missed-out-on/

Tomsett, J. and Uttley, J. (2020) *Putting Staff First: A blueprint for revitalising our schools.* Woodbridge: John Catt Educational Ltd.

Wiliam, D. (2013) *Principled Curriculum Design.* SSAT (The Schools Network) Ltd.

Wiliam, D. (2014) *Principled Assessment Design.* SSAT (The Schools Network) Ltd.

Wiliam, D. (2018) *Creating the schools our children need: Why what we're doing won't help much (and what we can do instead).* West Palm Beach: Learning Science International.

Willingham, D. T. (2017) *The Reading Mind: A Cognitive Approach to How the Mind Reads.* San Francisco: Jossey Bass.

Worth, J., De Lazzari, G., and Hillary, J. (2017). *Teacher Retention and Turnover Research: Interim Report.* Slough: NFER.

Young, M. (2014) *The Curriculum and the Entitlement to Knowledge.* Cambridge Assessment Network. https://www.cambridgeassessment.org.uk/Images/166279-the-curriculum-and-the-entitlement-to-knowledge-prof-michael-young.pdf